MAGGIE AND PIERRE
& THE DUCHESS

MAGGIE

AND

PIERRE

&

THE

DUCHESS

AKA WALLIS SIMPSON

BY

LINDA GRIFFITHS

PLAYWRIGHTS CANADA PRESS
TORONTO

For professional or amateur production rights, please contact:
Michael Petrasek, The Talent House
204A St. George Street, Toronto, ON M5R 2N6
416.960.9686, michael@talenthouse.ca

LIBRARY AND ARCHIVES CANADA CATALOGUING IN PUBLICATION
Griffiths, Linda, 1956-, author
       Maggie and Pierre & The duchess / Linda Griffiths.

Includes two plays: Maggie and Pierre and The duchess.
Issued in print and electronic formats.
ISBN 978-1-77091-178-9 (pbk.).-- ISBN 978-1-77091-179-6 (pdf).--
ISBN 978-1-77091-180-2 (epub)

       I. Griffiths, Linda, 1956- Duchess II. Title. III. Title: The duchess.
IV. Title: Maggie and Pierre and The duchess.

PS8563.R536M34 2013 .   C812'.54 ·   C2013-904409-4
                                                    C2013-904410-8

We acknowledge the financial support of the Canada Council for the Arts, the
Ontario Arts Council (OAC)—an agency of the Government of Ontario, which
last year funded 1,681 individual artists and 1,125 organizations in 216 communi-
ties across Ontario for a total of $52.8 million—the Ontario Media Development
Corporation, and the Government of Canada through the Canada Book Fund for
our publishing activities.

 Canada Council Conseil des arts
for the Arts du Canada

 ONTARIO ARTS COUNCIL
CONSEIL DES ARTS DE L'ONTARIO
50 YEARS OF ONTARIO GOVERNMENT SUPPORT OF THE ARTS
50 ANS DE SOUTIEN DU GOUVERNEMENT DE L'ONTARIO AUX ARTS

 Canadä

 Ontario
Ontario Media Development
Corporation

CONTENTS

MYTHOLOGIZING THE WILDERNESS: AN INTRODUCTION TO LINDA GRIFFITHS

After a long and difficult gestation involving, collectively and individually, Maria Campbell (Metis author and activist), Linda Griffiths (actor and writer), and Paul Thompson (theatre director and founder of the iconic Theatre Passe Muraille), *The Book of Jessica: A Theatrical Transformation* rises in 1989 like a phoenix from its combustion of creative egos and cultural sensitivities. Ultimately containing the play *Jessica*—written by both women, initially acted by Griffiths and directed by Thompson—a searing and sensitive exploration of its artistic process, and a play about the play, *The Book of Jessica* dramatizes Griffiths's brave streak through the gauntlet of personal and political revelation. This journey—riveting and raw, intelligent and passionate, realistic and fantastic—informs her best work.

Linda Griffiths creates drama that articulates, whether with painful effort or blinding clarity and usually with excoriating humour, the existence of a wilderness in all of us and the desire to explore it, the dangers hidden within it, the necessity of knowing it without destroying it, of harnessing its power and understanding how to use it. In a note prefacing her play *Chronic* (2003), Griffiths says, "Only in nature, inner and outer, is there some balance. Only in the inner forest is there light." Yet her work is neither therapeutic nor particularly consoling. It is disturbing, unnerving. It wakes you up. And keeps you awake with what she identifies in *The Book of Jessica* as "the theatre gods." Often referred to as her fabulist instinct and contextualized by her own production company, Duchess Productions, as "a dance between the personal, the political, and the fantastic," this non-naturalistic impulse (harnessed to real story) is her particular connection to the unknown, the unseen; it is her larger spiritual home. In *The Book of Jessica*, that wavering need—complicated by Catholic guilt and Celtic history—clashes with Metis Maria's own mixed-race background, deconstructing and re-constructing both women through an urgent poetry that remains unique in Canadian drama.

In his introduction to *Chronic*—an "ecodrama" that joins the twentieth-century idea of "illness as metaphor" with twenty-first-century cyber technology to explore various "pathologies" of modern life—Jerry Wasserman declares accurately that Griffiths's "central figure is almost always a woman engaged in a struggle for power." As well, "Almost every play features some kind of alien invasion or visitation." And Griffiths's women, he goes on, either wrestle with or channel the power of that other dimension. The eponymous Jessica in the 1981 play confronts the fierce animal spirits of her people. Perpetual flower child, Margaret Trudeau (*Maggie and Pierre* 1979)—ferocious and funny—paces the cage of modern feminism, political imperatives, and counter-culture fantasies. Wallis Simpson in *The Duchess* (1998) cavorts with a chorus of aristocrats and dancing jewels. The pregnant SHE and her impregnating HE in *The Darling Family* (1991) wind themselves tight as tops in their neurotic Never Never Land. The hilarious *Game of Inches* invokes baseball fantasies to spotlight the complications of real-life relationships. Poet Gwendolyn MacEwen meets with her dark invaders in *Alien Creature* (1999).

Allowing the other dimension always involves risk. The tourists in *O.D. on Paradise* (1982) watch their fragile self-images crack under the solar microscope of a Caribbean getaway. *The Darling Family*, ingeniously subtitled *A Duet for Three*, relentlessly examines the forces that come into play when their big event occurs. Indeed, the piece is an experiment in minimalism and anonymity appropriate for underlying tragedy as startling in its effect as Hemingway's "Hills Like White Elephants" or Joan Barfoot's *Dancing in the Dark*. Petra in *Chronic* must confront her virus, animate and insistent; Gwendolyn MacEwen in *Alien Creature* must deal with the creative-destructive power of her poetry through the mask of magic. The comically deadbeat, youthfully inept filmmakers in *Brother Andre's Heart* (1993), animated by their addiction to *Star Trek: The Next Generation* and characters from *The Clan of the Cave Bear*, flesh out their fantasy lives with a heart heist (based on an actual news story) of the holy relic from Montreal's famous basilica, only to realize that genuine sainthood involves genuine work.

These are all versions of Griffiths's "theatre gods," that other dimension that can be identified with the wilderness inside major (often female) characters, as a spiritual quest, theatrically undertaken.

How do Griffiths's theatre gods operate?

The Book of Jessica embraces a process that is relentlessly vulnerable, refusing to censor difficult emotions. Rather than being uncomfortably confessional, it encourages us all to explore the deep wells of our fears and desires, our shame. From the unpredictable "sibyls" of improvisation comes the play *Jessica*, filled and fraught with theatre gods from Maria's Metis heritage and her own harrowing story. Coyote, Bear, Unicorn (representing the mythic and mongrel powers of white culture), Wolverine, and Crow—actors in evocative animal masks—guiding spirits and dangerous tricksters, battle through image transits and the music of transformation to change her life. Arousing all the senses, full of urban tragedy, spirit rivalries, and sharp comedy, *Jessica* makes its theatrical mark—one that, with stunning variety in form and subject—distinguishes all of Griffiths's work.

How are Griffiths's plays classic?

In her own words: her characters are huge and carry on a mythological struggle. She complains in *The Book of Jessica* that "we can't even do the Greeks or Shakespeare anymore because we don't believe in anything." Myth-making is one response to our fundamental need for significance. In that sense, the figures in Griffiths's drama strive for something larger than themselves, but they must look inward for it ("only in the inner forest is there light"). In this sense, they are contemporary and relevant, but because their stories stretch beyond ordinary life, they are also classic. Accomplished and popular, historical and mythic, dramatically innovative, Griffiths's plays *Maggie and Pierre* and *The Duchess* exemplify the classic in her work.

Based on the unlikely May/September union of Canada's dapper, game-changing Pierre Trudeau and Margaret Sinclair, wide-eyed flower child from Vancouver (the two rather longingly compared to Jack and Jackie as the Canadian version of Camelot), *Maggie and Pierre*, subtitled *A Fantasy of Love, Politics and the Media*, is brilliantly theatrical, cantering through the enigmatic and tempestuous marriage of the first Canadian couple, who are benignly but quizzically and sometimes angrily interrogated by the journalist Henry. Written by Griffiths with Thompson, played with superb theatricality, this one-woman extravaganza engaged all of Canada (including Maria Campbell) in its dynamic conversation.

Griffiths is a wide-eyed Margaret clutching her rose, the porcelain-perfect face (a variation on the Virgin Mary milkiness that so angers Maria in *The Book of Jessica*), ready to soar into ecstasy the moment she jumps off that cliff. Is the vitality she so rivetingly embodies sabotaged by a naively false notion of complete freedom? She is the idealistic poet of lifestyles eager to hitch her wagon to his visionary statesman but all too often mired in the mud of hypocritical political manoeuvrings. Griffiths's Pierre is savvy and full of sass. Calculatingly, both emperor and clown, drugged on love, he rides the success train like a pro. But he also breaks.

Griffiths takes Trudeau-inspired political slogans of the day along with Margaret's counter-culture enthusiasms and works them into the doll-house crucible of *Maggie and Pierre*. The torrent of current events—revolving around the Quebec situation and the larger Canadian identity, along with their transforming impact on these figures—is distilled into the fragmented voice of each character in a kind of overheard consciousness, his quick scattershot and her inner editor, eventually developed as the highly effective technique of "thoughtspeak" in Griffiths's richly layered and exuberantly relevant take on the Victorian "woman question," *Age of Arousal* (2007). Wit, humour, and lightning-quick transitions pace *Maggie and Pierre* like a fine racehorse. This kind of precision is progressively defined and refined in Griffiths's drama until by *Age of Arousal* it has crescendoed into a profoundly satisfying rhythmic orchestration.

As *Maggie and Pierre* progresses, Pierre is overcome by the psychic struggle between his personal and political life. He must deal decisively with the October crisis and a bored, depressed Maggie about to fly the coop. Henry feels betrayed by a PM who has plunged a country with an inferiority complex into a worse inferiority complex. The big fight happens to a backdrop of Reason over Passion, acrimony equally distributed. Pierre urges Maggie to stay and fulfill their immortal destiny. She flees to her life of sex and drugs and rock and roll, a disco doll encaged in her own frantic narcissism. By the 1979 federal election, she admits to being "the woman who gave freedom a bad name." Falling on his knees, confessing to Henry that, locked in his own gender, he doesn't know how to respond to her, Pierre embodies the tragedy of the oppressor who can never be free.

Seared by his involvement with them, Henry has the last word. He's "the guy who can't stop watching" and has nothing to offer except "two small giant figures… like you hold in the palm of your hand." Here is the large mythological struggle lit by an inner wilderness that characterizes Griffiths's major work.

Comparing Griffiths as Margaret Trudeau with her portrayal in 1997 as Wallis Simpson, Duchess of Windsor, is to appreciate the range of her theatrical imagination. Many trace elements of *Maggie and Pierre* can be found in *The Duchess*. Both women leap into the rarefied atmosphere of powerful men at a time when power was considered decidedly unfeminine. Maggie and Pierre are divided along the fault lines of reason and passion. Wallis is told that her intelligence is unreliable because her reason is connected to passion.

Playing Simpson, Griffiths is satiny smooth, sleek, and sly, cavorting pantherlike with Noël Coward and the English nobility, romancing her besotted but feckless Prince Charming, Edward VIII, into the fairy tale they both seem to need. But she is also the wild woman breaking out and letting go, a dominatrix snarling at his weakness, fingers ready to claw at the billowing, bejewelled elegance of her gilded cage. As director Layne Coleman suggests, she is the scream at the heart of the century, her bleeding ulcers erupting like the chaos of war through the veneer of the "civilized" world. This murderous Black Queen swinging her bloody axe tantalizes her audience: "I'm a witch, a Fascist. It was my fault, the whole century." In an earlier version of this play, Wallis raves, "They want to murder me." Who? The royal family, "The whole horse-faced, jug-eared lot of them." Typically, Griffiths's ebullient humour carries its cargo of human striving and failure, poignantly and passionately female.

The play flashes quickly back to how she got here from there. As several critics have noted, Wallis is transported—much like Jessica—to past events in her life by a chorus of spirits unique to her story: members of the British aristocracy and the jewels she wore (actors mincing like "runway models"). Glitteringly deceitful, this fabulist element of the play is variously sinister, consoling, devious, and hilarious, casting Wallis's blunt American pedigree into fairy-tale context, adroitly mixing high and low cultures: "Once upon a time there was a poor southern girl, with hair as black as ebony, lips red as blood, skin as white as snow, and a face like a plank." With that ever-vigilant theatre opportunist Noël Coward ironically stirring the pot, these elements combine to bubble up an alternately dynamic and deadly concoction of farce and tragedy in a myth of ancient Britain with roots stretching all the way back to legendary Albion.

Griffiths's writing sizzles, as angry as it is funny. Triumphantly self-aware, Wallis wants to "wake them all up. From graves and palaces, wars and revolutions." Jauntily the chorus chants doom. "Once upon a time there was a Prince… a prince of hearts, he dined on tarts…" Mother Goose fantasies of royal recklessness darken to graver predictions such as popular uprising and war. In a few deft strokes, Griffiths creates the tensions that stretch the royal family on its rickety rack of monarchial absolutism. Edward, heir to the throne, will be the peoples' king, wanting, increasingly, to know the real England in Stonehenge and Druid circles and periwinkles in the wood. His royal parents, fiercely opposed to this failure of nerve consider him "terminally high-strung." Queen Mary elaborates on "the constitutional advantages" for Edward of "an intact English Rose," while they all discreetly slaver over Wallis's reputed expertise in Fang Chung, the erotic arts of China.

Through the banter and the frolic and the kinky sex, Wallis and Edward ultimately see a new world in each other. She rouses and arouses him, shakes him out like Lady Macbeth with a whip in the bedchamber, riding him into modern monarchy, and enjoying enough royal privilege along the way to cause her to confess to Coward that she has become "Wallis in Wonderland."

The Duchess is shot through with the seductions of style. Naked ambition wrapped in classic femme-fatale glamour, Wallis exudes jazzy glitter. As in *Age of Arousal*, where a "lightening of the (colour) palette," "a sprinkling of sparkle," or a shiny fabric can suggest "a whisper of modernity" about the Victorian proto-feminists of that aptly labelled erotic opera, Griffiths understands the theatrical currency of the visual. It is style that the royals finally recognize as Wallis's popularizing force. By comparison they are seen as "plodders." In the Fascist Germany that becomes the couple's desperate refuge, even Hitler—working on an Impressionist painting that Wallis recognizes as a map of the world—acknowledges the power of "beauty, blood, and style." When he discovers Wallis is wearing fake jewellery, he summarily dismisses them. Later in the Bahamas, bereft in their final refuge, Edward demands she make him an elegant home where they can "invite the world to dinner."

When Edward tells Wallis he will abdicate to be with her, she sees only disaster, guilt, and blame. With him gone, the kingdom will disintegrate. Is her power empty, her ferocity rootless, an enchanting tale? Becoming the irate voice of the crowd at Edward's impending abdication, furious at being denied their new king, the fabulous jewels turn against her. The Black Queen is also the woman who starts wars. At Edward's abdication, cursed by the archbishop and cast out by Queen Mary, Wallis relegates royalty to the fairy-tale realm and prepares to enter the void of Nazi Germany. Hitler plans to conquer England but she knows that is impossible because "everyone in that country is a character in a tale already told."

As Wallis's physical pain increases, so does her fantasy life. At first beguilingly vacuous, it becomes malevolent. A brief respite against encroaching darkness, the Bahamian party spirals down to Edward's irreversible cancer and the ultimate selling of her irresistible, treacherous jewels, the auctioning off of her royal English fairy tale. He dies, leaving her to understand that she is stuck in the murderous twentieth century and love has come too late.

Once again, Griffiths hitches the tough political business of the world—Hitler's dreadful force—to a magical mystery tour that is driven by her theatre gods and rooted in a female wilderness. The playwright has characterized Wallis as her Hedda Gabler, both women trapped in a world too small for them, disastrously thwarted in their ambitious, narcissistic all-consuming drive to create themselves. What one might call the exaggerated expressionism of *The Duchess* can be seen as an appropriate depiction of a woman who has not fully incorporated the wilderness within. What Griffiths explores in both these plays is the combustible mix of male and female as public persona, of love and politics played out in the civic arena, the bedroom, the palace, and the Parliament.

Consistently, Griffiths dramatizes the powerful mythic pulse driving her people while celebrating the human spirit—both wild and weak, fearless and flawed—that animates the myth. In doing so, she elevates Canadian drama to an imaginative level also occupied by such playwrights as George Ryga, Sharon Pollock, Judith Thompson, and Daniel MacIvor. Playwrights who understand, in the current artistic climate of stereotyping and small vision, theatre's particular potential to outstrip the one-dimensionality of docudrama, sitcoms, and television's relentless reality shows. These playwrights use the unique resources of theatre to dramatize the psychology, history, and mythology embedded in the human stories it can most vividly tell. In her work for the theatre, Linda Griffiths examines, fearlessly, the individual detail of particular story while courageously and creatively imagining the larger picture.

—Patricia Keeney

Patricia Keeney is a poet, novelist, arts critic, and professor of English and Creative Writing at York University.

MAGGIE AND PIERRE

by Linda Griffiths with Paul Thompson

MAGGIE AND PIERRE:
A DIALOGUE WITH THE WHOLE COUNTRY

*You told me you wanted it all... four thousand miles of
diversity, contradictions, and space.*
—Pierre Trudeau, *Maggie and Pierre*

Near the mid-seventies, Linda Griffiths and seven other idealistic young women rented a station wagon, filled it with props and
sleeping bags, and proceeded to present theatre in cities, towns,
and villages throughout eastern Canada. Bezumba Theatre per-
formed their shows in ad hoc venues to people of all shapes and
sizes, recording twenty thousand miles on the beleaguered vehi-
cle. They were in the vanguard but were not alone. In fact, they
would become part of a surge of young companies that shared this
same impulse for discovery, both of themselves and of the country's inhabitants. As artistic director of Theatre Passe Muraille, I
was deeply caught up in this movement, and early plays such as
The Farm Show and *1837* did much to help set the tone. It seemed
inevitable that Linda's path and my own would cross.

This happened in Saskatoon in the summer of 1975, where I
ended up sharing some TPM collective techniques for a co-produc-
tion with 25th Street Theatre in a play about the Saskatchewan
scene entitled *If You're So Good, Why Are You In Saskatoon?* Linda

was with the company and she took to the new way of working brilliantly. Her research was rich and passionate and her improvs would focus on the singular, the unusual, and, occasionally, the magical. She seemed fearless as a performer and I remember to this day her piece on the spirit of the Bessborough Gardens, where she melded history and gargoyles into a seamless narrative. In many ways it set the mould for our future collaborations.

Fast forward to Montreal in 1978, where Passe Muraille was taking on the whole separatist phenomenon. Between us by that point Linda and I had done at least five more collectives— either with each other or separately—but none prepared us for the challenge of presenting a play in our mangled French for the *indépendantiste* audiences of Théâtre d'Aujourd'hui. It was called *Les Maudits Anglais*, a favourite insult of the English by French Quebec. It would call on all the political savvy and theatre survival techniques the company could muster. In one scene Linda played a kind of puppet version of our prime minister. It was startling to me because she revealed an aspect of Trudeau that nobody had yet noticed: his feminine side. "If you can do Margaret half as effectively, you have yourself a one-man show," I proclaimed. Linda required a year of thinking about it to agree.

I now know why. Looking back on the process, I see how she had to summon every aspect of herself for this play: the protofeminism of the Bezumba Company, the magic of the gargoyles, the politics from *Maudits Anglais*. And that was only the starting point. Our rehearsal room became research central for a crash course on political science and Jungian psychology. Every idea was tried in an improv. Characters were created, loved, then thrown out because they didn't fit the story (goodbye, Mrs. Michener); strong political personalities were brought in to argue every side of a policy; a lawyer came in to explain why we might be sued; the characters of Pierre and Margaret came into the room and started to weave their own particular spells. We found a model for our journalist while having lunch with Henry Champ, who told us everything we needed to know, then warned us against the cliché of a trench-coat-wearing character—his own trench coat hanging beside him, along with his clichéd hat. We stopped rehearsals for a week because the play was lacking Ottawa credibility. Linda travelled there and dug into the whole scene with amazing resourcefulness, infiltrating the Governor General's Ball and dancing with Trudeau himself. "You must be some sort of student," he mused charmingly when she tried to explain the play she was creating. Linda returned and the play took over. Her research was so rich that she could improvise sequences forty-five minutes at a stretch. Theatre was telling us what to do. We still had to edit, add brilliant sets, costumes, lights, and sound. But somewhere deep inside her, the play was already there.

And what was this play? Just like what the Bezumba's wanted, it was a dialogue with the whole country. It previewed in the Backspace of Passe Muraille (too long, but a revelation), then went out of town to the welcoming arms of Saskatoon, where this hungry audience told us what we needed to know about the play—both by their reactions and their after-show comments. We learned that every audience felt that they owned Trudeau. By the time we returned for the Toronto opening, the play had a life of its own. It was critic-proof, but it had its own rules of care and maintenance. That looked after, we were along for the discourse. Montreal, Vancouver, Edmonton, Calgary, Blyth, Victoria, Halifax, Winnipeg, London, back to Toronto at the Royal Alex, and off-Broadway in New York City. Each city responded to the show in a unique and measurably different way. But they all needed to talk afterwards. About themselves, about the country, about… they needed to talk. Thank you Bezumbas and all the early companies.

—Paul Thompson

Paul Thompson is a playwright, director, and the founding artistic director of Theatre Passe Muraille in Toronto. He has been named an Officer in the Order of Canada and was awarded the Governor General's Performing Arts Award for Lifetime Artistic Achievement. He is the co-author of *Maggie and Pierre* with Linda Griffiths.

DANCING WITH TRUDEAU

It wasn't my idea. Paul Thompson and I were working on *Les Maudits Anglais*, and I was fooling around with this Pierre Trudeau character; it felt cool to pretend to be the prime minister. The rest of the cast would laugh when I did him, and Paul would hop up and down, so I kept bringing him into very scene. I can still see Thompson's face floating in front of me with its dwarf beard, "That's it," he says, "that's your one-person show. You do both of them, Maggie and Pierre." His words had a ring to them, like what the devil says to catch you. I said there was no way I was doing a one-person show. Too lonely.

Six months later we were in rehearsals for *Maggie and Pierre*. I was doing what Paul called "research." Reading books, listening to tapes, watching the news. The Maggie character was coming along, idealistic and innocent, sexy and narcissistic. But the Pierre character was stiff as old cardboard. I could do a few funny turns, including a pirouette, but the real person was far away from me; I felt totally out of my depth. I wanted to do more than some caricature, I wanted his breath, his mind, and suddenly I wanted his soul. To go that deep I had to find some way to meet him, then I'd steal his soul and give it back on the stage. If you do something like that, you always have to give back tenfold.

I read that the fall parliamentary session began with something called the Governor General's Ball and somehow I was going to get to that ball and dance with Pierre Trudeau. He would be as I imagined him to be, as millions imagined him to be, even though at the time they were sick to death of him. The romantic Trudeau would reveal himself, then his evil twin would show up—not evil, but dry and professorial. The Trudeau I intended to meet would be the Trudeau of legend. The sensual lips would curl quizzically, the high cheekbones would gleam, his tux would fit perfectly—with some small outrageous touch all his own—and he would dance divinely.

I found out that the ball was held in October and immediately started scheming. I had nothing to wear, but my boyfriend had been left with a trunk of clothes from his ex-girlfriend, and in that trunk was a dress. A vintage black-lace gown. It was very old, probably from the twenties, and the lace was torn in places, held together with a rhinestone pin, but it had a kind of beauty.

Shoes were a problem, but shoes are always a problem. I travelled to Ottawa by bus with the dress in a plastic bag. The ball was in two days and I had no concrete plans about how to get in.

I'd already done a couple of small trips to Ottawa, forming relationships with a few journalists at the Press Club. I was amazed by how much they gave away, how desperate they were to talk, how raw were their emotions. You just had to ask about the Trudeaus and out poured toads and flowers, jewels and lizards. She was a delicate rose, lost and deceived, she was manipulative, she was dumb. He was wise, arrogant, enlightened, dangerous, a patriot, a hypocrite, a champion. Rumours abounded about his sex life. A conservative MP told me Trudeau was gay and regularly had it off on the train to Montreal with the conductor. According to him, they'd cram themselves in the washroom and do naughty things.

My special friend at the Press Club was a young journalist who actually knew a couple of actors. He was very discouraging about the ball. He said it wasn't a big deal, that none of the high-level newspeople went, it was just a gossip-column thing. But if I really wanted to go, he could get me in with the reporters. The hitch was, they were only allowed to stay for the first dance, then they had to leave. I had to dance the first dance with Trudeau.

The afternoon of the ball, I went to Parliament for the first time in my life. I walked through the grey stone arches and stared at the Gothic carvings of grapes and leaves. Gargoyles with satyrs' faces were tucked erotically in high corners. I went to the visitor's gallery and looked down on my Parliament, at the bright green of the desk blotters, a startling colour in the middle of all that dark wood. Mostly paunchy old men slouched at their places. I counted the women. Was that one? Maybe two? I could have touched them. There was no glass wall then, there was open space; you could have thrown a spitball, or a bomb. I watched Trudeau. He'd just lost what many called the Disco Election. Maggie ran off to New York with the Rolling Stones, dancing in a disco frenzy the night the votes came in. I wasn't one of those young people who automatically loved Trudeau; I was vaguely critical. He had been fun at first, but then he'd suspended civil liberties and that was bad, and then there was something about wage and price controls. But as I was watching him these matters became immaterial. I saw how he lightly touched the House, hovering in his chair as if he barely sat, as if he was a visitor himself, as if he was about to wink at me like Sean Connery in some cheesy movie and say, "It's all bullshit, but what's a man to do?"

"Dance with me," I said to him silently, then decided to write him a note. I scribbled on a piece of scrap paper from my purse: "Dear Pierre Trudeau. You don't know me, but I will be at the Governor General's Ball with the reporters, but I am not a reporter. I have a very strange request. Would you dance the first dance with me? I have long dark hair and I will be wearing a black dress. I will explain all this later." I wandered through the halls, an Escher-like maze of stairways and archways, looking for someone official. I finally found a security guard and handed the note to him. 'Would you give this to Pierre Trudeau?" He nodded calmly, as if he did this kind of thing all the time. I'd done all I could do, now I had to get dressed.

I was staying with actress Nicky Guadagni, who was about to play Ophelia at the NAC, and I think the ingenue nature of the role influenced her fashion advice for the event. As I held up the dress for her to see, I noticed more rips in the lace, but Nicky said it didn't matter as she curled my straight hair, trying to give it a natural twist. When we got to the makeup she said, "Not too much. You're young, that's what you've got going for you. He'll be surrounded by old people, his wife's just left him and he lost the election. Just do lipstick and a bit of powder."

Rideau Hall was a great dark mansion. With the light spilling out from the windows, it looked like something from a black-and-white horror movie. Limos were pulling up to the door. I saw a group of reporters huddled together in the chill, waiting to be let in. I knew none of them and none of them were dressed up. They looked at me and then glanced away. I was very quiet; I didn't want them to talk to me. I was separate, a spy. Through them I heard that dinner came first, then the dancing.

The reporters and I were led in as a group and on the way we passed the empty ballroom, cordoned off by a purple velvet rope. It was a classic Victorian room, with large gilt framed pictures of former governors general and their wives, and it was lit by lights shaped like candles. The huge chandelier shed a nasty top-light and you had to wonder if it looked just as bad when it had been lit up with real candles. In the anemic glow, with the chandelier dangling overhead, the ballroom looked so British and colonial.

Instead of being seated with the rest of the MPs, we were put into another room and made to eat separately. I was beside myself. This was it? I would eat with a bunch of reporters, stand behind a purple rope, watch the first dance, and go home? I didn't have much hope that Trudeau had gotten my note, so I quickly scribbled another one, saying the same thing, but this time more desperate. "I am with the reporters but I am not a reporter. If you don't dance the first dance with me I'm going to be kicked out. Can you help? I have long dark hair and I'm wearing a black dress."

It turned out we were to eat first, isolating us still further. As the reporters, once more carefully escorted as a group, went to line

up for the buffet, I held back. I ducked into the beautifully dec-
orated washroom and hid in a stall till I thought they'd finished,
then, with my note crumpled in my hand, I joined the line for the
MPs. I looked around, trying to see some cabinet minister I might
recognize, but no one looked familiar and time was running out.
I peeked into the official dining rooms, all laid out in linen and
silver, but I couldn't be too obvious and Trudeau was nowhere
to be seen. The man in front of me looked nice and French. I
had nothing to lose. I asked him if he knew Pierre Trudeau, he
laughed and said he did. Would he give him a note? He said he
would. And so a second note may or may not have been passed
on to the leader of the loyal Opposition.

Finally the meal was over and we were herded to the foyer
just beside the ballroom. We bunched together behind the velvet
cord while the MPs drifted in. All I could think of was that it
looked like the high-school prom except everybody was older.
Then Trudeau entered. I stared, willing him to notice me, but
not a glance did I get. Almost immediately the first dance started.
Trudeau led off with the governor general's seventeen-year-old
daughter. It was over. I stood watching the scene, knowing that
in a few minutes I would be gone. The dance ended, I prepared
to go. Then Trudeau started walking towards us. He looked right
at me, smiled, and extended his hand over the velvet cord. I took
his hand and entered the ballroom.

There is a photograph of this moment, which one of the society reporters must have taken. There she is, a young woman in a
black-lace dress, hyped-up, overwrought, with popping eyes and
skin stretched tight over the kind of smile that shows all your
teeth and gums. An almost patriotic excitement exudes from her.

There's a rather odd Indonesian purse dangling from her arm, but the shoes don't look so bad.

I babbled. Of course I babbled. I remember saying something like, "Thank you, oh, thank you, they were about to kick me out." I hope I didn't say, "You saved me," but maybe I did. Somewhere I was thinking, "He's so little. He's just a little taller than me."

I heard Pierre Trudeau say, "I'm sorry, I couldn't dance the first dance with you…"

"Oh that's fine, I understand, I'm just so happy that you… that you're… that you got my note."

"Now, what's all this about? Why are they going to 'kick you out'?"

The quizzical smile was on his lips and revealed to me in all its wonder was the part of him that loved to engage. He was curious, he was interested, he listened. It was as if every word I said was a jewel, as if he was massaging me from the inside. I had the feeling I could tell him anything. But I couldn't tell him anything, now could I? Guilt began to tug at me, like a Parliament gargoyle standing on my shoulder, whispering in my ear. I wondered if Mata Hari ever felt guilty.

Trudeau took my hand and led me deeper into the room. We started to dance as I was still trying to explain.

"I'm writing a play about… Ottawa and…"

"About Ottawa, that's a pretty strange subject." Gentle irony. Oh God.

"Yes it is, and I wanted to come here and get an idea… you know, research…"

I could feel his body underneath the suit. He held me lightly. There was dandruff on his shoulders.

"Is there anyone here you would like to meet?"

I giggled. I couldn't help it. "No, that's fine, it's just so wonderful that... you're that... you did this... that you're you..."

It wasn't just one dance, it was four or five dances. I wasn't used to this kind of pseudo-ballroom dancing. It reminded me of when my father taught me to dance. I'm in the rec room and my mother is playing the record player and my father is teaching me to dance. I tell him nobody dances that way anymore.

I giggled again. Trudeau smiled again and bent his head fetchingly to one side. "What are you laughing at?"

"I'm just not used to dancing this way..." I wanted to squeeze him and feel his muscles.

"You intimidate me when you laugh."

"I intimidate the prime minister of Canada!"

Really, he was the former prime minister, even then, but people were always forgetting to say "former." I think it was because he won again later on, and after that no one believed it was ever over. "The prime minister's casket is travelling on a train from Montreal to Ottawa," the former prime minister...

He was very relaxed everywhere but his shoulders.

"You have soft hair." Said quietly, into my ear, his cheek at my hair. And then came the bandying back and forth of flirtatious phrases.

"That's a lovely dress you're wearing."

"Oh, it's full of holes."

"But in all the right places." Who could get away with that?

I wanted to tell him about the play, about my dreams for it, about my thoughts of the personal and the political and how they connected. Thank God I didn't. The more kind and courtly, the more lightly sexual he was with me, the worse I felt. How many times during those four or five dances did I try to find a way to tell him? I was dancing with the Pierre of legend, but he could turn on a dime. What if the persona that emerged sometimes on the evening news showed up? A kind of skull look, his pockmarks pitted like potholes on the moon, the bags under his cheeks grey purple, brilliance sharpened as the proverbial blade—ready to skewer girls like me.

But it was the vulnerability that got me, his precious, stunning vulnerability; if I really played him I would have to show that vulnerability. And that is what he would hate me for the most.

We seemed to dance for a very long time. I kept expecting him to leave; I knew he would have to mingle. Then I remembered he'd come alone, that here were a familiar group of people with few surprises to offer and that I, at least, was a surprise. It occurred to me, with a funny stab of pain in my heart, that he might be lonely. With that thought, I started to breathe him in. I tried to see the world from behind his eyes. I began to feel bound, as if to some unspoken pact of honour with him. In the play that was to be, I would rise above base instincts, both mine and the audience's. There would be no cheap laughs, or hardly any. This was especially noble, as a good laugh is worth a lot in my business. But I now felt responsible to him and for him. Responsible to his vulnerability—and they ask about the secret of charisma.

It was all coming to a close, I could feel it. "Is there anyone else you would like to meet?" He said this generously, a man used to giving favours. I looked around the middle-aged promsters, ready to go home before nine. "No," I said, "no one else." He said he had to speak to some people. I said I understood. He gave me the number of his secretary and I wrote it down on the crumpled note that had somehow been passed on to him. It took me years to realize that maybe I wasn't the first young woman who'd ever been given that number. "If you ever want to give me a call, here's my secretary's number." "Oh thank you. Thank you so much."

He then called over an aide-de-camp in a white uniform with large gold epaulets who strode over quickly at some kind of signal. "This is Captain St. Laurent, he'll take care of you and make sure" (with one of those smiles, his silver blue gaze locking mine) "that you don't get 'kicked out.'" He embraced me, kissed me on both cheeks. I fumbled the French kiss and then danced with Captain St. Laurent for a while.

When I finally got back to Nicky's, she was waiting for me. She's told me too many times later, "I didn't have to ask, it was all in your face," and she does a rather cruel imitation of me looking like I've just had a vision of the baby Jesus.

The response to the play was overwhelming to me. There was the trick of it, a woman playing both characters—and Henry, who everybody forgets. The Maggie character was the centre, the star, but the real trick was Trudeau. In spite of a few slightly cheap laughs, I think it is the Trudeau of legend who is in that play. And when I was so tired on tour that I wanted to hop a plane to Mexico to get out of it, I would try to imitate his ability to engage with an audience as if each person was a precious jewel. There was also the sheer joy of his lovely adult male ego, which had always had a certain androgyny. I found that the middle finger on my right hand would want to pierce the air in people's faces at regular opportunities. I took to shrugging a lot. So who stole whose soul?

For a long time I had a recurring dream. I dreamt I was dancing with Trudeau and trying to find a way to tell him about the play. I couldn't do it. Then, not so long ago, I had the dream again. I was dancing with Trudeau and I told him about the play, and he understood, and it was wonderful. But just as he walked away, I realized I hadn't told him about the second act. In the second act the Pierre character gets down on his knees and prays. As tears fall down his cheeks, he prays for strength, for the country, and for love. He admits he hit her.

I'm in my dressing room after the show, still in my Trudeau costume with the fake rose in the lapel. This guy who's seen the show comes in. "I love the way you really got Trudeau. There won't be any tears at his funeral."

I was shocked. The man was as vile and bitter as a betrayed lover. And I realized the entire country had danced with Trudeau. Some felt dropped like old high-school flames, and some still felt beloved. It doesn't matter how it went. What we felt for Trudeau was true love, and true love never goes away. It stays in the heart and mind, forever confused and faithful.

—Linda Griffiths, 2001

PLAYWRIGHT'S NOTES

Because of the way *Maggie and Pierre* was developed in rehearsal, certain production aspects were a more integral part of the play than is usual. Imagine a work process that demanded the "look" of a character in a given scene before it could be written, and you will see the kind of contribution designer Paul Kelman has made. Imagine analyzing a personality through an extensive study of her favourite rock-and-roll music, where scenes were written from the inspiration of that music and you will understand the involvement of Al Higbee.

There were something like thirteen costume changes in this one-person extravaganza. They needed to be expertly and quickly executed. Myles Warren, working invisibly in awkward backstage circumstances, created a flow essential to the production.

Maggie and Pierre previewed in the Backspace at Theatre Passe Muraille in Toronto, Ontario, on November 30, 1979. It opened in the Mainspace at Theatre Passe Muraille on February 14, 1980, with the following cast:

Henry, Maggie, and Pierre: Linda Griffiths

Director: Paul Thompson
Set and costume design: Paul Kelman
Lighting design: Jim Plaxton
Stage manager: Myles Warren
Design assistant and master carpenter: Bob Pearson
Assistant to the lighting designer: Steve Allen
Audio research and production: Al Higbee
Initial script preparation: Judith Rudakoff, Myles Warren, and Kit Dawson

PRODUCTION HISTORY OF MAGGIE AND PIERRE

Spring 1979
Paul Thompson begins rehearsals for a play about English people going to Quebec, *Les Maudits Anglais*. During improvisational sessions, Griffiths keeps doing a Pierre Trudeau character. Thompson says, "That's your one-person show, you do both of them." Griffiths says she doesn't want to do a one-person show.

Summer/Fall 1979
Griffiths and Thompson begin improvisational rehearsals for *Maggie and Pierre*. Instead of taping the improvisations, Thompson uses a Passe Muraille employee, Kitten, as a live stenographer. During this time, Griffiths makes three trips to Ottawa. On the third, she gets into the Governor General's Ball.

December 1979
Maggie and Pierre receives its first workshop production in Theatre Passe Muraille's Backspace. The production includes a two-level set with a ladder backstage, Rolling Stones songs for the transitions, and thirteen quick changes—from Maggie's bathing costume to full political suit for Pierre, to Henry's coat and hat. In the second act, the costume images are reduced to a more basic

look for the three characters, excepting the signature disco outfit for Maggie near the end of the play.

January 1980
A slightly shorter version receives a full production, complete with standing ovation on opening night. The play immediately seems to engender more publicity than most Canadian plays— perhaps encouraged by a character based on themselves (Henry), the political media also write about it. This bypasses the quota on Canadian entertainment coverage.

Spring 1980
Maggie and Pierre tours to Vancouver, playing a sold-out eight-week run at the Vancouver Cultural Centre. Margaret Trudeau sees the play, arriving with a friend. After the show, the stage manager, Myles Warren; his wife, Judith Rudakoff; Griffiths; and a couple of friends go out for beer and pizza with Margaret. As was fitting, Griffiths paid the cheque.

Fall 1980
Maggie and Pierre tours to the Centaur Theatre in Montreal, Theatre Calgary, and Edmonton. In Edmonton the show plays at the University of Alberta, starting a trend for independent producers to produce it when regional theatres are not interested. All these producers make money.

Fall 1981
The demand for *Maggie and Pierre* grows and the search begins for another actress to perform and tour the play. Toronto actress Patricia Oatman is chosen and Paul Thompson begins rehearsing

her in. When Griffiths sees Oatman do the show, she thinks Oatman's Trudeau is perhaps a little better than hers. Oatman receives wonderful reviews and plays Winnipeg, Victoria, Saskatoon, Thunder Bay...

Spring 1981
Maggie and Pierre plays Ottawa, not at the National Arts Centre, but at an Ottawa high school auditorium. Rumours abound that cabinet ministers and high-level bureaucrats are arriving incognito. Pierre Trudeau does not come, as he is busy hosting Ronald Reagan, who arrives in town during the run.

Summer 1981
Maggie and Pierre returns to Passe Muraille as part of Toronto's International Theatre Festival, run by Shane Jaffe. Ticket demand is at such a premium that there are fistfights in the lobby to get seats. Shane Jaffe and Paul Thompson conspire to move the show to a larger location. Shane finally says, "The hell with it, let's go to the Alex."

Summer 1981
Shane Jaffe and Paul Thompson (with Theatre Passe Muraille) do the unheard-of. They rent the Royal Alexandra Theatre for five nights, hoping people will just show up. They do. Griffiths is the first woman to play a solo show on the Alex stage since Ruth Draper. *Maggie and Pierre* paves the way for other local plays to be produced by the Mirvishes and everyone got dinner at Honest Ed's Steak House.

Summer 1982

Paul Thompson wants to keep the show going but Griffiths is flagging. He decides that if someone else plays Henry, and if that someone is Griffiths's boyfriend, she'll keep going a while longer. Patrick Brymer is contracted to play Henry on a tour of southwestern Ontario. In southwestern Ontario, the show is usually referred to as "Pierre and Margaret."

Summer 1982

Garth Drabinsky shows interest in taking *Maggie and Pierre* to New York in an off-Broadway theatre. He partners up with Norman Kean, who had made money as one of the producers of *Oh! Calcutta!* (a few years later, Norman Kean shot himself and his wife). For some reason, Drabinsky thinks someone else should play Henry. Hoping that this might make it easier for someone else to eventually slip into the show, Griffiths agrees. Eric Peterson is contracted to play Henry in a limited run at the Phoenix Theatre in New York. Eric is a great Henry, but the split is not good for the play. Something about the power of one playing three is broken.

Fall 1982

Maggie and Pierre begins previews at the Phoenix Theatre. No one tells the company that in New York critics come to the previews. During previews, the play is very uneven and finally comes together on opening night when hundreds of critics have already seen it. The critical response is dire, except for Clive Barnes, who unfortunately no longer works for the *New York Times*. The general response is that an upstart is suggesting that their stars are bigger than our stars—and they're not. This translation of the story to the American Myth is a disaster. In a never-to-be repeated exercise in Canada/us cultural relations, *The Globe and Mail* prints the *New York Times* review of *Maggie and Pierre* verbatim, without comment. Frank Rich begins, "Poor Canada…" and goes on from there.

Late Fall 1982

John Sayles, an independent filmmaker, sees Griffiths's picture in the *Times*, winces at the review, sees the play, and auditions her for his new film, *Lianna*. Paul Thompson and Eric Peterson return to their work in Toronto and Griffiths goes to Hoboken to film the title part of the movie.

Spring 1998

The Playwrights Union of Canada asks Griffiths and Thompson if they will do *Maggie and Pierre* as a benefit for the organization. They agree. Myles Warren is again stage manager and Judith Rudakoff gets student volunteers from York University to help out. *Maggie and Pierre* is again mounted with a one-level set and thirteen quick changes for a two-night run. There is a big laugh when Henry/Griffiths says he's doomed to tell this story over and over again.

1998

Based on the success of the benefit, Susan Serran, then artistic director of Theatre Passe Muraille, decides to mount a revival. *Maggie and Pierre* plays again, and Thompson directs. New audience members arrive, many who have barely heard of Pierre Trudeau and have never heard of Maggie. They have barely heard of the Stones. *Maggie and Pierre* enjoys another sold-out run, people judging correctly that Griffiths is about to put away her disco pants forever.

Fall 2000

Pierre Trudeau dies. Public mourning is intense and overwhelming. The country is insatiable for stories of Trudeau. The media remembers the girl who did a play about Trudeau and his wife…

More or less, we're all afflicted with the psychology of the voyeur. Not in a strictly clinical or criminal sense, but in our whole physical and emotional stance before the world. Whenever we seek to break this spell of passivity, our actions are cruel and awkward and generally obscene, like an invalid who has forgotten how to walk.

—Jim Morrison, *The Lords and the New Creatures*

CHARACTERS

Henry
Margaret Trudeau
Pierre Trudeau

ACT ONE
SCENE ONE

HENRY DOESN'T WANT TO

HENRY is discovered on the telephone in a state of some agitation. Refusing a job has always been hard on him.

HENRY   No. Absolutely not. That's my final word. I'm not writing about those two any longer. I know what you want. You want exposé, you want the story behind the scenes, you want smut. Well, go on, admit it. Look, I know everything there is to know about those two. I'm just not telling anybody. No, and that's my final word. No.

He hangs up the telephone, begins pacing back and forth, and talks to himself.

I'm not writing about those two any longer because I'm not interested… And even if I was interested, I wouldn't write about them… for personal reasons.

He turns to the audience.

You see before you a man obsessed, tortured, a walking-cliché journalist… except I've heard lately… I don't know if you've heard this… that it's a cliché to talk about being a cliché… but how else to describe a world still filled with deals, deadlines, and the scent of stale election promises in the air? Haunted by two giant figures with two giant pairs of eyes… Maybe if I wrote about them one more time I'd get them outta my head! Right… No… So what, eh? I mean, so what? So a man marries a woman, they have a couple of kids, they break up, she goes a bit wild, he loses his job, he tries to get it back. So why write about that? What's the difference between them and anybody else? You want to know what the difference is? The one that I figured out anyway… that everybody watched… Millions… that close, like voyeurs, or like the circus… Hooray, hooray, hooray. Pierre Trudeau marries twenty-two-year-old bride. Baby Justin born Christmas Day. Margaret Trudeau hospitalized for nervous breakdown. Pierre Trudeau refuses sympathy election based on separation… Maggie boogies with the Stones and writes exposé book… Joe Clark wins election… J. Pierre Trudeau resigns as leader of the Opposition, and on and on. You see, I wrote those headlines—me—and because of that and everything that happened, they can never be two small figures to me, like the kind you hold in the palm of your hand. They're huge, they're giants… two epic characters, and they carry on a mythological struggle. They're King Arthur and Guinevere, and Clytemnestra and Agamemnon, and they play out our pain way up there. There's something at the centre of the story, something that affected everybody deeper than they're willing to admit… Who's going to tell it but me? Right? Right.

He picks up the telephone.

All right, ya son of a bitch, I'm going to do it… Ya, but my way. What I saw, what I see.

He hangs up.

Funny, it's as if I'd been there at every turn and twist along the way… watching. You know, she was nineteen years old, and it was one of those bright white light days in Tahiti, with the waves gently lapping against the raft…

SCENE TWO

TAHITI

On that fateful day, MARGARET *is sunning herself, clad in a classic bathing suit.*

MAGGIE   I can't believe it… Here I am in Tahiti, at the Club Méditerranée, I'm getting a half-decent tan, at least for my kind of skin, and I'm here with my parents. I don't know what to do with my life. I could open a school for retarded children; I could join the Revolution and the Black Panthers. Or just drop out and do lots of really good drugs… Who's that? Who's that water skiing? Hey, he's pretty good. Is he trying to impress me? Of course he is. Men are so transparent. How old is he? Twenty-five? No, maybe a little older. I knew it. He's coming over…

PIERRE   Hello. What's a beautiful girl like you doing here all alone?

MAGGIE   Oh, God. Cutting parental ties, trying to decide what to do with my life. I'm in a state of confusion, but then confusion's the name of the game, so it's all right. What are you doing here?

PIERRE   I'm reading *The History of the Decline and Fall of the Roman Empire* and deciding whether or not to become prime minister of Canada.

MAGGIE   Sounds really exciting.

PIERRE   It's not a dull book. You should read about the bacchanalian rituals.

MAGGIE   Read about them. I've been there.

PIERRE   That sounds like a long journey. How much farther do you want to go?

MAGGIE   Forever. And you…? I want to be world-renowned, to shape destiny, to be deliriously happy. You might say, I want it all.

PIERRE   I want to be world-renowned, to shape destiny, to be deliriously happy. You might say, I want it all.

MAGGIE   What did you say?

PIERRE   I'm sorry, what did you say?

MAGGIE   You heard what I said. Do you mean it?

PIERRE   Just watch me.

MAGGIE   No. Just watch me.

PIERRE   If you're serious about this, I'm sure you'll be inter-
          ested in exploring the challenges of snorkelling with
          me tomorrow at ten o'clock.

MAGGIE   Maybe.

PIERRE   Maybe, you're serious?

MAGGIE   Maybe I'll go snorkelling with you, tomorrow at ten
          o'clock.

          She exits, having won the day.

SCENE THREE

'68 CONVENTION

          PIERRE *appears waving to an ecstatic crowd. They
          are chanting, "Tru-deau, Tru-deau, Tru-deau."*

PIERRE   Getting off at the railroad station… a spontaneous
          demonstration, thousands of hands reaching out
          to touch me, rip off pieces of my clothing, women
          throwing themselves at my feet. People laughing,
          crying, kissing, fainting. It's not a leadership cam-
          paign; it's more like a coronation!

          Cheers are heard.

I wonder how many people have felt this kind of reinforcement, not for their philosophy or ideas, but for their personality, perhaps even for their body...

It's not right. This is the kind of emotionalism that fostered Fascism. I want to tell you that the government is no Santa Claus.

Cheers are heard again.

It's hard to resist... And there will be one Canada and that Canada will be progressive! We have no need to become a great military power, then let our power come from within, from a just society.

Cheers are heard again. He executes one of his famous pirouettes.

I know what I will do with this Liberal Party. I will take this right winger and this left winger and stop all the endless squabbling. I will become like an alchemist and forge out of everyone's opinion a shining wheel of a party, a wheel that will go ever forward, and just a little to the left.

He exits amid cheers.

SCENE FOUR

HENRY'S POLITICIAN

HENRY enters just as PIERRE leaves, looks after him for a moment, then addresses the audience.

HENRY   You know, when I first came to Ottawa, I expected it to be like those TV press conferences. You know the kind... politicians on one side, journalists on the other, and everybody's on the attack. You could never imagine these people in the same room with each other. I arrived on Parliament Hill to find a small town of about three hundred people. The doers and the watchers all mixed in together exchanging information, drinks, and sometimes even wives for mutual benefit. And I learned the fine lines of conduct where you can drink with a man one night, write about him the next, and look him right in the eye the day after. You're never friends and you're never enemies. Gossip was king, not politics. As for the rest, we were a pretty boring small town… I mean, most of the MPs were still staying at the YMCA. I'd watch Diefenbaker and Pearson hacking and hewing away at each other like two old gladiators. The biggest thing that happened was the flag debate. Dief calling on the old powers of the British Empire only to find out that they didn't give a shit any longer. We had nothing going for us except a certain cynical, satirical sense of humour about how ridiculous we were. And we'd cast those longing glances across the border to you know where. Then, all of a sudden, out of the clear blue sky, comes this guy… and he's sexy and classy and brilliant and athletic and liberal-minded and adventurous! New York was jealous… and the bugger spoke French! Guys like that didn't usually dirty their hands with politics. He was a member of the ruling class that chose to rule. We were flattered. And because he was sexy and classy and athletic… we became sexy and classy and athletic.

You're from New York, are you? Too bad… Pierre Trudeau? Oh, yeah, just another typical Canadian. French? Sure, most of us are *bilingue parfait.* Sexy? Classy? It's the long winters.

And you couldn't understand a goddamn thing the guy was saying… Rows of journalists down at the library… Who the hell is Loqueville? Or is it Tocqueville? Has anyone read *Buddhism and the Natural Man?* It was fantastic. I loved the guy.

And all the while I was watching him, enjoying him, I had this almost eerie sensation that things were going to get unusually complicated… I just didn't know how.

SCENE FIVE

---

17 MAGAZINE

> MARGARET *is pensive in her good-girl dress. At first, she is removed, as if telling someone else's story. Later, she becomes more desperate to be where it's happening. A* VOICE *criticizes her every thought.*

MAGGIE   It wasn't as if she was timid or afraid. It was as if, as she went towards what was expected, she went just a little bit too far, beyond the delicate point of naturalness, giving everything she did and said a strange air of falsity that she herself questioned at every turn.

VOICE   Margaret. You're trying just a bit too hard.

MAGGIE   No, it's what they want… Hello, Daddy. I've got your pipe and slippers. Hello, Mr. Jenkins. Daddy, is it all right if I sit on Mr. Jenkins's lap? I'm glad you think I'm pretty as a picture. I have to go now to meet the captain of the football team… I…

VOICE   Margaret, look around. No one else is dating the captain of the football team.

MAGGIE   No one else is still acting like me. No one else is still dressed like me.

Her dress comes apart and drops to her knees. She heaves a sigh of relief.

VOICE   Margaret, put on your blue jeans.

MAGGIE   I don't think I like these kinds of clothes. I like things with a bit of lace on them… Ohhhhh, I understand. Oh, yeah… They're for sitting on the ground with your legs open wide, they're for… *(chanting)* "We're not going to class, we're not going to class"… They're for… *(singing)* "There is a house in New Orleans, they call the rising sun…"

VOICE   Margaret… look around.

MAGGIE   Where'd everybody go?

VOICE   Late again, Margaret. No one goes to university any-more. They've all gone to Exotica, to Greece and Africa.

MAGGIE   All right, I'll go too. I'll lose my middle-class clean-liness there…

VOICE   How are you going to get there?

MAGGIE   With two thousand dollars worth of Dad's money, but
            I'm not going to spend it… It's off to Morocco and
            Marrakesh, really strange food and really strange…

VOICE   Margaret, you still sound like a phony.

MAGGIE   I'm trying… Living a communal existence where
            you pretend you don't need any privacy at all. Of
            course, I'll make love to you, I'm not afraid of my
            body. You're not afraid of yours and I'll even enjoy
            it, and I'll make love to you and you and you and
            you… Standing in a gold-domed square with some
            guy going, "Nyahhhhhhhhh"… How come all of a
            sudden everybody looks like something out of a Bible
            school picture? How come they think I'm the Virgin
            Mary? And what's worse, how come I think I'm the
            Virgin Mary? This is too freaky, too weird… Back
            to BC and Canada… Granny's cabin in the woods.

VOICE   Margaret… you're not even a real hippie, you're just
            thinking about what a pretty picture you make wan-
            dering around the trees.

MAGGIE   First, what's a real hippie? Second, yes, I am think-
            ing about that, but I'm thinking on the inside too.
            You can be outside and inside at the same time,
            you know…

VOICE   Answer the telephone.

MAGGIE   Mom? How did you find me...? Heyyyy get real,
               I don't go out on dates anymore... Who? Pierre
               Trudeau? That's for real.

SCENE SIX

LES SNOBS

*PIERRE speaks as though discovering this person
himself, almost surprised at his own actions, phys-
icalizing every step along the way. He begins by
zipping up a black leather jacket.*

PIERRE   Imagine a man—no—a child, about three years old,
               and his parents are telling him to go to bed, and he
               says, "No, you're wrong." Why? "Because the book
               I'm reading now is more important to my future
               development than the fifteen minutes more you want
               me to sleep." Imagine him then seeing that look
               on his parents' faces of unquestioning authority...
               I'm right because I'm right because I'm right... And
               imagine him resolving, for the rest of his days, to
               fight that look. Five years old, hearing somewhere
               that fresh air is good for you, up goes the window.

               He begins to breathe deeply.

Six years old, the 5BX plan, self-discipline, twenty minutes every day. Why? To be strong. What for? To fight. Who? I don't know yet, but I'm going to find out very soon…

Sitting in the classroom… the Battle of the Plains of Abraham. The students are looking maudlin, the teacher's getting out her handkerchief, and there's a general air of cloying sentimentality in the room. "And so, Montcalm lost his life, Quebec lost her heart, and we went down the drain to the dastardly English." Hurrah for the English!!! You should have seen the look on their faces… What are we talking about? Winners? Losers? If we had won, would we not be cheering for ourselves? Who fought the best battle? The English. We deserved to lose. We'll always lose, so long as we drown in waves of emotionalism. "Don't think, Pierre, just feel?" Exactly! If thought is an enemy, then we are fascists...! I've never known if I say these things because I really believe them or because I just like bugging people...

Brebeuf College, becoming a member of an elite group called Les Snobs... Enemies of righteousness. We dress up in German uniforms during World War II, knock on people's doors and tell them they've been arrested. Why? To make them examine their own sense of safety...

Sick of Quebec, sick of empty nationalist whining, off to Harvard Law School, and it's Law and Society and Man. How does it all fit together? And where do I fit in? Maybe Paris, the Sorbonne, my attic apartment, my Mercedes downstairs, six o'clock in the morning, a freezing-cold room, a basin of ice water... all down a naked body. Why? To be strong. What for? To fight. Who? First myself, and then... anyone who dares me...

Off to find adventure, danger, the war zones... China, Vietnam, Palestine. I get arrested. Why? To find out what it's like. And then it's the internal journey of the soul, and so it's Buddhism and chanting and yoga. All right, body, soul, mind, all tuned, all tingling...

Come on… What don't I know? Come on… Quebec? I'm always thinking of Quebec. A dictatorship to fight? We are our own dictators. You dare me? So, it's back to Quebec, the Asbestos Strike, thousands of cheering workers… "It is the time to take up arms against the oppressors; now is the time for cataclysms!" Practical politics, Pelletier's kitchen… Lévesque, Marchand, Pelletier. What about Quebec? What about federalism? Where do we fit in, where are we going wrong? Writing treatises against the Liberal Party. They're only interested in perpetuating their own power, it has no… Come to Ottawa? You've got to be kidding? The Liberal Party? I don't think they would take me. They will? A challenge is a challenge. Why not?

SCENE SEVEN

GROUSE MOUNTAIN

MARGARET *is behind a screen, rushing through the motions of preparing for a date. The absurdity of the situation is beginning to dawn on her.*

MAGGIE   Oh no! I look like a Barbie doll. Why did I let them do that to my hair? Cheryl, will you bring up that stuff… All this fuss, for what? Just another corrupt politician. I was even going to put that junk on my nails. I can't believe it. I gave up all this materialistic

crap a long time ago, matching handbags, high-heeled… shoes.

A moment of appreciation quickly squashed.

Look at this dress, we could have lived for six months in Morocco for what this cost. It's immoral.

She struggles with the dress, then stands with it over her head and laughs.

It's like a viewfinder made of lace.

The dress slips down over her head and she looks at herself in an imaginary mirror.

I don't know why I'm so nervous, I guess if I want to. Don't answer the doorbell. And cool the giggling, all right?

She opens the door.

He's so little; he's just a little taller than me. I can't look at him. Oh no, he's offering me his arm.

Thank you. You're wearing a cravat! Oh, no, I just don't know anybody that wears cravats... And a month ago in Morocco, we weren't wearing anything at all. Oh, great, it's the kind of restaurant my parents go to. No, no, that's fine. He's pushing my chair in, I hope I don't land on my ass... Thank you. I'm pressing my knees together so hard my thighs hurt. What did I take in university? Political science, I took politi... Bad choice, Margaret. Did you really win a contest for having the most beautiful legs in the world...? He thinks I'm an idiot. How strange, it's as if I'm falling into his eyes... One hundred percent charm and all real. He's trying to tell me something... that he's shy too! It's as if every word I say is a jewel...! It's like he's massaging me from the inside! I can tell you anything. What were my courses like in university? Well, Pierre, they're about a whole generation of people just stepping back and saying, "Hey, hold on." They're about people looking at war and money and corruption and politics and saying, "Look, there's got to be a better way." About everybody feeling a part of a whole movement, going, "Don't trust anyone over thirty!!!"

She realizes she's put her foot in it.

Basically, Pierre, I just really do a lot of dope... He's laughing. He's not shocked at all. He likes me talking like this. Is he an old man or what...?

Flash, flash, flash... Autograph hunters...

Margaret Sinclair. No, that's all right, you can take my picture. Oh, God, I hope I look all right...

Flash, flash, flash, flash...

Funny, signing those autographs, he looked like Clark Gable. And a while back, talking politics, he reminded me of that guy with the khaki shorts that used to follow me around Morocco. And just then, ordering the wine, he looked like Ricardo Montalbán. He changes, frame to frame to frame. It's like watching television! He's making a funny little old-fashioned bow that matches the cravat. It's so cute. He's asking me to dance. "Of course, I'll dance with you…"

They dance to the Rolling Stones's "Wild Horses."

Do you know what this reminds me of? One night when I was thirteen years old, my mother and father and I went down to the rec room, and my mother played the record player and my father taught me to dance. Dancing with you is like dancing with my father.

PIERRE   You're making me feel old.

MAGGIE   I'm sorry. You could never be old.

PIERRE   I'm two years older than your mother.

MAGGIE   You'll never be old… I can feel his body underneath the suit. Strong, but not like a football player's. Flexible, like a dancer's.

She giggles.

PIERRE   What are you laughing at?

MAGGIE   Oh, I'm just not used to dancing this way.

PIERRE   You intimidate me when you laugh.

MAGGIE   I intimidate the prime minister of Canada! Hey, you wouldn't be intimidated by a string of Mack trucks.

PIERRE   You have soft hair.

MAGGIE   He thinks I have soft hair... How much do I want? Don't blow it, Margaret, just open your eyes wide and make him think of hyacinths. It's like flowers in springtime and every atom in my body feeling alive... No, exploding... It's like really good acid and being on mescaline for eight hours and sitting up in a tree, thinking you're a bird... Come on, Pierre, baby, let's dance all night!

PIERRE   Margaret? Don't you think we should be going? Everyone's left.

MAGGIE   I didn't even notice. Isn't that a line out of some movie?

PIERRE   I don't know. I don't often go to movies.

MAGGIE   Are you going to take me right home?

PIERRE   I'm a well-brought-up boy, I get my eight hours sleep. I have a busy day tomorrow. Yes, I suppose so.

MAGGIE   I mean… where are you staying?

PIERRE   At the nearest CP hotel… It's Canadian… It's a joke…

MAGGIE   Far-out, Pierre. That's really good. Well, I guess it's good night.

PIERRE   Come and see me if you ever get to Ottawa. I'd be interested to see what happens to you. Give me an enchanting evening.

          They kiss and PIERRE *exits, leaving* MARGARET *with a last thought as the music swells.*

MAGGIE   It's like… kissing a dried rose.

SCENE EIGHT

PIERRE PERTURBED

PIERRE and HENRY are in a murky bar. Both are slightly uncomfortable, aware of the unusualness of their situation.

PIERRE   Well, Henry, you're probably wondering why I've brought you here to this out-of-the-way bar in this out-of-the-way part of Ottawa.

HENRY   Yeah, yeah, to tell you the truth, I had been wondering why you brought me here, seeing as how I've only spoken with you about twice.

PIERRE   You seem to be a man of some discretion... have experience in certain areas, and I was in need of advice in a hurry... and you were available. A personal matter. Three triple Scotches, please.

HENRY   But you don't drink... All right, if you're in need of a little advice, sir, go right ahead. Believe me, I'm all ears.

PIERRE   I'm thinking of marrying a twenty-two-year-old flower child.

HENRY   Is she pretty?

PIERRE   Don't be banal.

HENRY   Don't you have someone else you can talk to, like a friend?

PIERRE   No.

HENRY   Sorry… How do you feel about her, or something like that? I don't know.

PIERRE   I don't know, I'm completely confused. I'm wandering around Ottawa in a kind of a daze. I keep thinking of flowers, but I can't remember what kind. I walk into Parliament and sit there facing Bob Stanfield, and last week he and the entire Conservative Party transformed into Margaret. I don't know, I think, perhaps, that it is time for me to embark on the ultimate relationship between a man and a woman—"I WANT A WIFE"—the sharing of a lifetime… I see little children playing in the street, and I think, I love children—"I WANT SONS"—and daughters. I feel experiences welling up inside of me such as I've never felt before—"I WANT SOMEONE TO FUCK ME SILLY"—I don't know, I'm baffled, I'm bewildered… I think I'm smitten.

HENRY   When guys like you fall, they really go, don't they, Pierre? Sorry, not funny. All right, you want to know what I think? Man to man, and not prime minister to journalist? I think it's a really stupid idea. Look, most of the women in the country vote for you because they think you're going to come through the bedroom window one night. I mean, think of all the votes…! Show me one of these May-to-September things that has ever worked out, just one. You got to watch yourself. She followed you to Ottawa, she's out to trap you. You can't trust a woman like that. Treat her like you treat the Cabinet… I think you should get up, go over to that telephone and tell the lady, "No go"… sir.

PIERRE   Of course, you're right. This is a crisis and I'm always good in a crisis. Thank you…

He picks up the telephone.

Margaret? Yes, I have been thinking about you. Yes, I do remember, it was wonderful… I wanted to discuss this entire marriage question with you… What do you mean, "When?" No, you don't understand, I mean, the dialogue must be completely revamped. "What kind of ring do I want?"… No, no, you don't understand, March is a terrible time for me… What about February?

He realizes what he's just said.

All right, what about February?

He hangs up the telephone with an air of rueful resignation. The lights fade to black.

SCENE NINE

___

HENRY'S QUESTION

HENRY becomes a Greek messenger, describing what is invisible to the audience by peeking behind a curtain, where the two characters, unaware, are continuing their tête-à-tête.

HENRY   Have... have you ever been involved in a key turning point in somebody else's life? You know what I mean? And forever after, no matter what else happens, you always feel involved? Well, that's what happened to me. I mean, it just doesn't make sense... Out of all the women that man could have had, why this one? I gotta find out...

So they're back at that restaurant, right...? Right. It's her I have to see. Hold on.

He looks behind the curtain.

She's beautiful as a Hawaiian flower... and she's a kook. That's it! He's afraid of becoming one of those grey-faced zombies that wander around Ottawa. She's supposed to balance the act. But the poor kid. Look at him.

He peeks again.

Oh, God! He's using every move in the book on her. It's a rout. "Why don't you pick on someone your own size, Trudeau?" She doesn't want to be a rose in his lapel.

He looks at her.

Oh, yes, she does! She's bringing out a few moves of her own. She's bringing out the old feminine wiles. "Watch out, Trudeau, this woman's dangerous!" She's using her youth against his age—no—he's using his age against her youth… They're doing it to each other… No, there's got to be a bad guy and there's got to be a victim…

He throws open the curtains and is about to interfere.

"Sorry… sorry… I… I didn't understand." I mean, sensitivity is not exactly my strong point. But, if you don't believe in that, what do you believe in?

SCENE TEN

DIPLOMACY

MARGARET *is dressing up again, but this time it is more natural to her. This is her first major social event as wife of the prime minister and she sees the possibility for evangelism in her new role.*

MAGGIE   Remember, you belong to the richest, healthiest, best-educated generation ever to hit the face of the earth, and there are millions of you. You're the first one of your kind ever to brave the bastion of their world. They're going to ask a lot of questions about what's been going on. Answer them all, be open, be vulnerable, don't let them get to you... Show them what a little love is all about. Remember, you're walking in there on the arm of the prime minister of Canada... You got him and they didn't...

The Governor General's Ball. It's like the high-school prom, except everybody's older. The world is run by mums and dads in their rented tuxedos and one long dress.

(to PIERRE) Don't worry, I'll be fine...

Hiiii... How are you? Do you know what it's like to be at a rock concert with fifteen thousand people and everybody's thinking the same thing... that some kind of change is bound to... happen.

Her conversation partner drifts away, uncomprehending, and she tries again.

Yeah oh... Oh... Thank you... Oh... you're very kind... Thank you.

Hiiii… How are you? Look, I know what happened to your son. He started to grow his hair long, didn't want to be a doctor, and told you to fuck off. Look, I know where that's coming from. I can help you.

Just… You think that everyone who smokes dope should be shot…! You're in Pierre's Cabinet?!?!?!

She runs to PIERRE *and they dance.*

Pierre, it's almost insulting. They… they think I'm one of them. They don't even see the difference.

PIERRE   You can't change everything in a single night. Just be yourself, just be natural.

MAGGIE   Why don't they realize they're obsolete?

PIERRE   Maybe they think you're obsolete.

She begins greeting heads of state.

MAGGIE   Mr. Chairman Mao, how do you do? Mr. Zhou Enlai…

Bowing a little uncertainly.

It's a pleasure, sir.

With confidence.

Mr. Kosygin. Mr. Nixon…

A moment of recognition.

Mr. Nixon. Queen Elizabeth…

She falls while curtsying.

Queen Elizabeth! Prince Charles…

A subtle gesture to the neck of her gown.

Prince Charles! Fidel Castro… Hi…!

Mr. Brezhnev, you know I went to Russia, and what bothered me about communism was the uniformity…

The lights dim and she hears distant rock music. It fades away. The lights come up abruptly. Her manner is now nervous and strained, overly formal.

I think that both our countries have really a lot to say to each other because they're both… cold…

Mrs. Meir, I wanted to go to Israel on my travels, but there was a war going on. I mean, people were dying. You're a leader, can't you do something…

The lights dim. The music returns, slightly louder this time. She loses herself in the music, her hips swaying in appreciation. The music fades. The lights come up. She searches for small talk.

Ohh, you know babies, they'll come along when they want to come along... Yeah, yeah...

Mr. Nixon, do you have any idea what you represent to the people of my generation?! To everybody?! You're a symbol of evil, of corruption. I know people that want to shoot...

The music returns, even more compellingly. She begins to dance. The music stops and she is shocked into reality.

How are Pat and... Trish...?

The music returns again. She is lost in the sound of sixties' electric guitars. She dances wildly, then recovers. The music swells over her exit line.

I'd like to tell you how much I've enjoyed meeting you all and how much I look forward to seeing you again in the near future.

ACT TWO
SCENE ONE

VISIONS IN THE BEDROOM

> MARGARET *and* PIERRE *are lolling around, letting their minds wander freely towards philosophy and the ways of the world.*

MAGGIE So now you have me, and the country, and everybody's rooting for you, what are you going to do with the "all" that you've got?

PIERRE I'm going to lead us all into the Golden Age.

MAGGIE Are you suffering from delusions of grandeur? Come on, it sounds as if you really believed in the Just Society or something. Look, I've been around enough politicians. It's okay to say something just to get in. Oh no… Oh no, you do, you really believe it.

PIERRE Here's the voice of youth, of optimism, a true daughter of the age of Aquarius. Margaret, of course I believe in it, it only makes sense. Why do they just want to touch me? Why is the whole country at my feet? Because I'm the first guy that ever walked into the House of Commons of this country with an idea... of how a whole society should work. Discussion, philosophy, and idealism creating a new order. We are on the threshold of a model of harmony and vitality for the world. Emmanuel Mounier writes of creative democracy. If we could only just believe in the possibility.

MAGGIE   But you're talking about Ottawa. Ottawa's full of frumps, they'd never understand what you were saying. I'm sorry, I know, you mean... change or the Revolution. Sure, I believe in it. I know lots of people that do. Sure, I have a vision of a world, but it's not practical. Sometimes, early in the morning, I can see it so clear. I see a wood, and sunlight streaming down, and people dancing naked like fauns, dappled sunshine on their bodies, fearless... but I don't know where they pay their taxes, or get their paycheques. But you know something about those people? They're totally free.

PIERRE   Well, all right, maybe there's a place for that in the Just Society. Maybe on sunny days, I should walk into Parliament and say, "Everybody out, all the MPs walk along the Ottawa River, take off your clothes, jump in, and make love to your wives, or your girlfriends, or someone." Just think how it would change the face of government... I want to know what happens if you put a communist, a socialist, and some guy from the Canadian Legion together in the same room and you make them fight it out… And you are the irrationality that perhaps somewhere along the line I have lost. You are the jolt of electricity that will set the whole thing going like some kind of ecstatic merry-go-round.

MAGGIE   I don't know… Why don't you call it something like the Psychedelic, Nutso, Let-It-All-Hang-Out Society.

PIERRE   You're being silly. It's the Reasonable, Yet Tolerant Society.

MAGGIE   You can't tolerate freedom!

PIERRE   All right. All right. Then it's the Reasonable, Yet Impulsive Just Society.

MAGGIE   I'm still a bit worried, and I think if you want to keep your little jolt of electricity, you'll have to chase your wife outside and we're gonna have to… DO IT IN THE ROAD!

She disappears, laughing.

SCENE TWO

OCTOBER CRISIS

HENRY catches PIERRE outside the Parliament Buildings. He and his tape recorder are worried about freedom.

HENRY   Sir, sir… Why are all these guys with all these guns running around?

PIERRE   Haven't you noticed?

HENRY   Yeah, I noticed. I wondered why you people decided to have them?

PIERRE   Well, what's your worry?

HENRY   I'm not worried, but you seem to be.

PIERRE   If you're not worried, then I'm not worried.

HENRY   All right, I'm worried. I'm worried about living in a society where you have to resort to that kind of thing.

PIERRE   It seems natural that if people are going to be abducted, we should take steps to protect them. What would you do if another minister were to be abducted?

HENRY	Well, that isn't the…
PIERRE	Is it your position that we should give in to the seven demands of the FLQ?
HENRY	No. That is not my position at all.
PIERRE	What is your position?
HENRY	My position is you don't give in to any of them.
PIERRE	But you don't protect yourself against the possibility of blackmail?
HENRY	Well, how can you protect everybody without turning the place into a police state?
PIERRE	You can't. But are you therefore suggesting we should protect no one?

HENRY is confused, then rallies.

HENRY	Right.
PIERRE	That's your position?
HENRY	Right… sir. Sir, sir… Sir, all right, maybe I explained it badly, but what you're talking about to me is choices, and my choice is to live in a society that's

free and democratic, and that means you don't have guys with guns running around in it.

PIERRE   Correct.

HENRY   And that means I might have to take the chance that a guy like you may be abducted.

PIERRE   Precisely. But I consider it more important to protect a democratically elected government, despite the protests of a few weak-kneed bleeding hearts who just don't like the look of a few guns. As far as I'm concerned, they can just go on and bleed.

HENRY   How far are you willing to go with that?

PIERRE   Just watch me.

SCENE THREE

WALK ALONE

Rain is falling and MARGARET *is trying to deal with security. She wants to rid herself of the feeling that she is being followed.*

MAGGIE   Mrs. Trudeau is being difficult today. No, no, I don't want to wear my galoshes. No, thank you, I don't want a rain hat or an umbrella. Don't you understand? I'm from BC. We like the rain. I just want to go for a walk by my…

She sees the security guards who will accompany her.

Oh no, the security guards don't have to come, do they…? Mrs. Trudeau is being difficult today, always a scene… Rain on my face, soaking through my clothes. These easterners will never understand. Oh no, one of them slipped! There's a place I like, down by the river, where the sewage dumps in. It looks like a waterfall. There's 24 Sussex Drive, way up on the cliff. They're watching me from the windows. And there's the spire of a church we don't even go to, and there are the Parliament Buildings, where he is. Funny, there's a kind of smoke that comes out of those chimneys, coloured like Faerie dust. Sometimes it's red and sometimes it's blue and sometimes it's gold. That's when he's talking. Political dust, and pretty soon it gets all over you and you've got an axe to grind or a position to defend. Hey! Hey, what's that? What's that movement on the water? It looks like wings, like wings beating underneath the water. Pierre would say, "No, Margaret. It's just the intersection of the wind and the rain causing that configuration on the surface." But I know it's wings. Is it possible to think if someone is always watching you?

Someone new watching, a new maid… Oh, boy. No. It's me. It's me… Watching Mrs. Trudeau standing just a little bit close to the water. It's me, all dressed up in my Yves Saint Laurent gown, a monument to good taste. It's me watching me, down by the river, a monument to bad taste. She wants me up there… She's beckoning…

Silently, she mouths the words…

No way…

SCENE FOUR

BOREDOM

The master and mistress of 24 Sussex Drive try to make it work.

PIERRE   Margaret, I'm home. As Heraclitus said, "You never walk in the same river twice," and that's what being prime minister of Canada is like. The only way to stay alive is to avoid their wish to define you. Am I a millionaire who's never worked a day in his life, or a dangerous communist? Québécois or a sellout? They'll never find out. I'm even enjoying the process of their disillusionment in me.

How perfect it is! The very things they loved in me six years ago, they can't stand in me now. I think what

	irritates them is the sight of a guy having a good time being prime minister. How I love it!
MAGGIE	I just got bored, just this moment. A frozen moment in time. Boredom came crashing through the ceiling and landed right there on the carpet like a piece of rotting meat. What am I doing with this man? We have nothing to say to each other…
	All the doors just opened, hundreds and thousands of them, the sunlight streaming through. Nothing is certain, anything is possible. I could be a journalist or an actress…
PIERRE	Margaret, what's going on?
MAGGIE	All the doors just opened!
PIERRE	Congratulations! I've been waiting for this moment to happen to you, when you stand there, full of self-confidence, and you watch all those possibilities open up. And you say, "I'll take a bit of this, a bit of that." Experience it to the end of your synapse. It's a wonderful feeling.
MAGGIE	I could be a nuclear scientist.
PIERRE	Of course, you could be a nuclear scientist.
MAGGIE	Or a rock singer. I could sing like Tina Turner.

PIERRE   Who?

MAGGIE   Tina Turner. She's a rock singer, Pierre. But I don't
              know, the light is blinding me...

              "Bee-bop, bee-bop-a-doo—Attica, Attica—Make
              love, not war—Freedom's just another word for noth-
              ing left to lose—Love is never having to say you're
              sorry—Freedom is, Freedom is—Drop in, drop
              out—Speed kills—One flew over the cuckoo's nest
              into the psychedelic sunset—Spaceship Earth, take
              off—Timothy Leary, where are you now?—Sing it,
              Janice—Ball and chain—I lost my ball and chain—I
              knew it was around here somewhere—You know
              what I mean, Jellybean?"

PIERRE   Margaret, are you all right?

MAGGIE   No, I'm freaking out. I think there's one thing, with
              all your knowledge, that you've never understood...
              human frailty.

PIERRE   You're right. I don't understand what it's like to live on
              your kind of edge. I have never freaked out... but I'm
              trying. I love you. And after those brown boxes full
              of important papers take me away, we could raid the
              kitchen for caviar or watch a late movie... *The Wild
              Bandit of Borneo* is on. You like that sort of thing.

              He kisses her and leaves.

MAGGIE	"Sometimes I feel like a motherless child…
	Sometimes I feel like a motherless child…
	Sometimes I feel like a motherless child…
	A long way from home, a long way from home."

As she sings each line of the song, another child wants to sit on her knee, until finally all three of her children are balanced there with difficulty. The lights fade.

SCENE FIVE

PRESS CLUB

HENRY and MARGARET are found in the journalist's hangout across the street from the Peace Tower. They have met in the street by chance.

| HENRY | I still haven't figured out how you managed to drag me in here to get drunk with you at the Press Club of all places. I was walking along, minding my own business… |

| MAGGIE | Henry, you said you wanted to get drunk. |

| HENRY | But not with the prime minister's wife! |

| MAGGIE | Come on, it was okay to have a couple of drinks with you boys on the campaign plane and on the trip to |

Cuba… Who am I going to hang loose with, Mrs. Michener? You always seem to have such a high time here.

HENRY   Yeah, it's a ball. All right, all right, it's not as if we were hiding from you or anything. The last time I saw you was at that dinner where you dropped mashed potatoes all down your…

MAGGIE   And you wrote about it. How is it you always remember these little details so clearly?

HENRY   I'm a good reporter… All right, all right, let's get the show on the road here. You know most of the journalists. Go right ahead, it's your night…

MAGGIE   Hii. Oh, hiii. Good to see you… Oh, you know, prenatal… postnatal depression, it's either one or the other with me… Politics! Oh, God, I hate politics…! I just keep telling him I wish he'd lose the next election…

HENRY   Margaret, Margaret, Margaret…! No, forget it, it's your night, go ahead…

MAGGIE   Ah, no, there's no trouble with that. Come on, he's got the body of a twenty-five-year-old… He does! Look, our sex life is great. Sometimes I dress up in this little garter belt and…

HENRY   Margaret, Margaret! There's a limit to "off the record."

MAGGIE   I've known these people for years, aren't they my friends?

HENRY   No.

MAGGIE   I know what you're talking about.

She breaks into a relationship with the camera. At first, it has a mind of its own, viewing her at its own whim. Finally, she wrenches the focus back to herself with a vengeance.

Those cameras, always on me. At first, I was really nervous, all those stupid pictures of me with that grin and… "I'm very happy to be married to the prime minister of Canada." And then they'd go away and I'd relax. And back again… "I'd like to tell you something about the man you may be voting for. He's not cold and he's not unfeeling. As a matter of fact, he has taught me a lot about loving…" No, I wasn't in the hospital for a cold or something.

I'm under severe emotional stress and psychiatric care, and I think that anyone else in that position should tell people and break the taboos.

She sings.

"Mrs. Perez, you are working hard,
with loving arms,
Mrs. Perez, both you and I know,
this is the shittiest job in the world,
Mrs...."

Naked on the beach... That's a funny question to ask, but I'll answer it. The trouble is my nipples... Have you ever breast-fed three children? No, eh? Well, your nipples go all brown and sticky on the edges... What do you want?

HENRY   Margaret, Margaret, Margaret! Whoa, whoa, whoa! Is that what you want? Haven't you figured this out yet? This is the snake pit. Don't trust them. Especially, don't trust me. I don't know why, but you're news, front page, just like your husband. You have got to watch out. The guy that interviews you has got to be his own censor. You'll say anything. It's frightening. Here, let me tell you a story. One day, I'm down in the library looking up some goddamn thing your husband said, something about Erasmus, and I come across Erasmus's letter to a young man going to court. It has advice in it like, "Confide in no one, yet seem to confide in all, never lower your position or become familiar, or you'll be hated for it." That's it, you're in court. Everybody gets weird when they talk about people in power. Do you have any idea what they're saying out there? That Trudeau screws RCMP officers under the bed, that you get off on it, that your kids were artificially inseminated… I'm telling you, this gets heavy, watch out!

PIERRE enters.

PIERRE   Margaret, I just received a call from my press secretary. I think it's time we were going home.

MAGGIE   Oh, just a few more minutes. Come on, I'm humanizing your image, and believe me, it needs to be humanized. It's okay, Henry is taking good care of me.

HENRY   Yeah. It's all right, sir. I'm keeping an eye on her. Don't worry about a thing.

PIERRE   You're keeping an eye on her? You'll exploit a fine person who happens to trust you. She'll speak freely to you, you'll write it down, she'll look like a fool, and you'll make money off her.

MAGGIE   No. That's not what he meant at all…

HENRY   No, no. It's all right, Marg, you don't have to defend me. It's just your husband's usual position on journalists. I think it's about time you realized, sir, that you've been better treated by the journalists of this country than any leader in the Western world.

PIERRE   Margaret, I'm really not interested in a scene, the car is waiting.

MAGGIE   I know this sounds terrible, but it's getting exciting
          and I want to know what happens.

HENRY   Your wife was starting to look forty-five years old.
          Tonight, look at her. Her eyes are glowing, her
          cheeks are pink, she's starting to look very… good.
          Just let the lady have a good time, will you?

PIERRE   Margaret, you're my wife and we're going home.

HENRY   Aha! I knew it. You're a dictator in the House and
          a dictator in the house. Let me tell you something.
          I don't'like the way you treat your wife, I don't like
          the way you treat journalists, and I don't like the way
          you treat the country.

MAGGIE   Hey… what are you fighting about? I like the way
          both of you treat me.

PIERRE   Speaking of the country… if I make a mistake, I'm
          responsible to twenty-two million people. Who are
          you responsible to? I speak issues and you write per-
          sonality. And if arrogance sells newspapers, then I'm
          arrogant. You're not a political analyst, you are paid
          to make me look like a fool, and I'm sorry, I don't
          enjoy being made to look like a fool.

MAGGIE   Stop fighting. You're making me like it.

HENRY   And who am I to criticize the great Pierre Elliott Trudeau? Just some poor schmuck off the street. You're the guy that's making a whole country feel stupid. You're giving us a worse inferiority complex than we had before. Now we feel inferior to you… You betrayed me! You betrayed all of us. You made us believe that some change was going to happen within the system, and then you shattered it. And that's why we're out to get you, because you personally betrayed me, personally.

MAGGIE   Henry, you're acting like a betrayed lover. Don't you understand? I'm the lover here.

PIERRE   And I'm the one betrayed. I came in here with new ideas all laid out. A latticework throughout the country for people to take hold and start believing in their own democracy. But I went a bit slow for you. You got scared and you retreated to your official position—"All politicians are crooks, they're just in it for another vote, they're trying to put one over on you." And you undermined the very basis of my credibility. You weakened the country I was trying to strengthen.

HENRY   No, you became corrupt. You… elitist!

PIERRE   You barbarian!

HENRY   You condescending, arrogant prig!

PIERRE   You dark vestige of a Neanderthal age…! Margaret,
            it's time to go.

MAGGIE   I think Henry's a little bit upset. Why don't you just
            let me talk to him by myself for a minute? You can
            just wait in the car. Okay?

            PIERRE leaves.

            Henry, men are so funny when they fight. Why aren't
            you supposed to talk about politics, religion, or sex?
            Because they're all the same thing. You're not going
            to print anything that happened tonight, are you?

HENRY   Margaret, is it possible that you're not as naive as I
            think you are? Are you trying to pull my strings? Is
            it conceivable that you are trying to get somewhere?
            Are you capable of ambition? Why am I in love with
            you? Why does the whole press gallery have fanta-
            sies of dashing off to save you from your husband
            or your children or something? I don't know, we've
            been protecting you for years. Did you do that? I
            don't know. I don't know if you really want me to
            print what happened tonight or not…

MAGGIE   Henry, how could you say such things to me?
            You have no idea how much you've hurt me. And
            whether you print tonight or not… of course… it's
            up to you…

SCENE SIX

THE FIGHT

PIERRE and MARGARET are discovered mid-argument. Imagined in the background is Joyce Wieland's quilt Reason Over Passion.

PIERRE   I received a bill from Creed's the other day...

MAGGIE   Now we're going to talk about money, but it's not about money, is it, Pierre?

PIERRE   I also wanted to discuss your relationship with our children. Justin mentioned to me the other day...

MAGGIE   You were speaking to Justin... You're using the children as spies! I thought I was paranoid, but I'm not paranoid enough for Ottawa.

PIERRE   I don't understand, we're privileged, you have everything you've always wanted, and that continues. I don't understand what could possibly be the matter with you.

MAGGIE   You're taking away my right to complain! I don't like the beautiful house. I don't like the beautiful job. I don't like what I see happening to you. You're starting to look like those cartoons.

PIERRE   We explained things to each other. I told you what
          our life would be like. We made a contract, an agree-
          ment. You've just got to be reasonable.

MAGGIE   Reasonable! Don't say that word, "reasonable." I'm
          not feeling very "reasonable" tonight. All I can see
          is that quilt with your motto, "Reason over Passion,"
          written right on it.

              *She mimes pulling the letters off the quilt and
              throwing them at him.*

          Here's an "R" and an "E" and an "A." Look at it! That
          woman made it for you as a joke. It's all purple and
          pink. It's got butterflies all over it. It's a joke about a
          silly man who lives by a silly motto. There's only one
          motto… "Be Here Now."

PIERRE   Is that what you've come to? Destroying a work of art?

MAGGIE   After all these years, I don't even know if you're disturbed
          or not. I want out. I WANT OUT OF CONFEDERATION. I'm
          sick, sick, sick to death of Canada. You know, John A.
          Macdonald made a railroad and we made a marriage,
          and he laid it from east to west, from sea to shining
          sea… You know, those guys at Confederation, they
          were drunk. They didn't know what they were doing.
          John A. put them up to it, and they signed this piece
          of paper, and we ended up with Canada. I'm sick
          of timidity and mediocrity, and Brights Canadian

Wine, fake Inuit carvings, and the Group of Seven! I'm sick of living in a ridiculous country, strung like a clothesline across the American border. Let's admit it; the Americans have always had more fun. Let's go there. No one was meant to live in this climate. Look at you. You're the epitome of a cold land. Let's go someplace warm, where people laugh and cry and hug and shout and dance in the streets. Come on, let's go. I'll pack the kids. We'll just go. Don't call anyone. Say it was all a mistake. Come on, look, we can still make it. I know you want to. Oh, please… Please…

PIERRE   You told me you wanted it all. You spoke of shaping destiny. Here is destiny. Feeling like a strong central column, springing from the guts of the land, with two arms outstretched, spanning four thousand miles of diversity and contradiction and space. You and I… and the country, involved in a struggle beyond ourselves. This is immortality. Stay with me, stay with me.

MAGGIE   You almost sucked me in again. You know, through all this, there's only one thing that seems to make any sense at all. Having fun… you remember? Having fun?

She dashes off.

SCENE SEVEN

ENTER MY EMOTIONAL WORLD

HENRY has reached the end of his rope. He wants PIERRE's soul on a platter. He enters Trudeau's private office.

HENRY You have to admit, when she went AWOL, she picked the best. It's become important to me, very important, to find out what he feels. I mean, I watched that guy for nine years. I see him more often than I see my own wife… But that's the story of my divorce and that's not this one… I mean, you're always trying to figure out what that tricky bastard's going to do next… and sometimes, you're even right. Except for this time. I haven't a clue. For some reason, I have to know if he even cares or not. I have to. Okay, so let's work it out… So… so… he's in his office, right? And you could pick many points of pain along the way, but let's be cruel. Let's pick one. Let's pick that weekend. So, he's in his office, right, and she's just left, and at some point or other, some poor flack had to make a phone call and say something like… "Sir, your wife has run off with the Rolling Stones. You know, the Bad Boys of Rock? Heroin, court cases… She's staying at the same hotel, same floor, and she hasn't mentioned you lately. We just thought you should know." I mean, what does a man, any man,

feel at a time like that? What did he feel? I have
to know…

PIERRE appears.

PIERRE   Well, why don't you ask me? Come in. Enter my
            emotional world. You may ask me any question that
            you choose.

HENRY   You're on. But I warn you, I'm going to dig deep…
            Okay, so that phone call happened. What was going
            on inside of you?

PIERRE   I was alone, she had just left, the phone did ring…

            *He reveals himself for the first time as he listens
            on the telephone, shaken, unable to hide the depth
            of the impact.*

            "No… I… I don't think there's any reason for a state-
            ment at this time, thank you." And amid all the pain
            and fear of being called a cuckold…

            He laughs.

            …there was an absurd sense of the perfection of the
            cosmic joke. I mean, a woman with half my intelli-
            gence has completely checkmated me. You have to
            give her credit. It's perfect.

HENRY	All right. So, it's kind of funny, I got that. But what else? What does a guy like you do when you're alone and in pain? What did you do that night?
PIERRE	Do you really want to know?

PIERRE closes the curtains and doors.

I wait until I am completely private…

He gets down on his knees.

"In the name of the Father, and the Son, and the Holy Spirit, amen. Dear Lord, I am in a state of such complete darkness that I have no idea where to turn, or what the answers are. I humbly beseech your aid in trying to find some way of strength out of this abyss. I also ask you to help me to keep from killing her when she gets back. In the name of the Father, and the Son, and the Holy…"

HENRY	Oh no. Not religion. Not a guy like you…
PIERRE	You know something, Henry? As we were going through all those horrendous fights, my wife was at my feet, and she was crying and screaming and wailing and literally banging her head against the wall, and I stood there, frozen, in the classic pose of man, locked in my own gender, not knowing whether to go to her and comfort her, or leave because it's too

personal to watch, or hit her, or what to do. And my dominant emotion was jealousy… that she could be so free. Perhaps that's the tragedy of the oppressor. There is a certain joy in it. Perhaps, for the first time, I feel a part of my entire society… The Old World is behind and the New World is a bit late in coming, and I ask, with all of us, "What are we going to do about marriage?"

He breaks the mood.

It's worth at least three white papers. Well, Henry, is that what you wanted to see?

Poor Henry. You never have known what it is you wanted to ask me. But I forgive you.

PIERRE blesses HENRY.

HENRY   How do I get out of here?

SCENE EIGHT

DISCO ELECTION

Raunchy rock music heralds the night of the May 1979 election. MARGARET appears in full disco regalia and begins to dance through the voices and the election results.

Rock music is heard between the voices.

WOMAN'S
VOICE   Listen, I don't care what she does, but why can't she keep her mouth shut?

MAN'S
VOICE   I find her totally unattractive. She's a flaky broad, a phony chick.

WOMAN'S

VOICE ⸱ She's put the feminist cause back five years.

MAN'S

VOICE Whenever I travel, people ask me about Margaret Trudeau. It's embarrassing. It's a complete drag. She's given Canada a bad name.

ANNOUNCER Liberals, elected two, leading in nine, for a total of eleven. Progressive Conservatives, elected one, leading in four, for a total of five.

WOMAN'S

VOICE You know, you can't just do what you want to do. Everybody has to have some responsibilities.

What kind of a mother could leave those beautiful children?

ANNOUNCER Nationwide standing. Liberals, elected in fifty, leading in fifty-six, for a total of a hundred and six. Progressive Conservatives have now elected fifty-one. They're leading in twenty-four, for a total of seventy-five. No change in Quebec, but in Ontario the Conservatives are making gains. And at least four cabinet ministers have gone down to defeat. From the bulk of the returns in from Atlantic and central Canada, the Conservatives have picked up a net gain of a couple of dozen seats in southern Ontario, and the decision desk is predicting a Progressive Conservative minority government.

The music stops.

Canadian Prime Minister Pierre Trudeau and his Liberal Party have been voted out of office.

MARGARET *stops dancing and turns to the audience.*

MAGGIE   All right. So… it's Margaret Trudeau, is it? Well, come on. Everybody's up there on their little soap boxes. Who's going to be the first one to stone the whore? That silly bitch… Well, come on… Is it the mums? The dads? The kids themselves? The marrieds, the divorced, the lefties, the righties? Well, come on, I'm the woman that's offended everybody. Oh, we're so together, aren't we, ladies? We're so on top of it all. We get up in the morning and send the kids off to school, then we get all nice and neat and go off to our really good day job, and we don't mind that all the bosses are still men, noooo… We're handling everything well—in control—we have no problems at all— Ssshhhh… We come home, pick up the kids from school, and we feed them a delicious dinner of soy beans and spinach—they've never had it so good. And then, hubby comes home and we have intelligent conversation with him—he's never had it so good. And then, at night, we get all foxy and *Vogue* magazine, and we go out and we flirt with the best of them, because we know that's still how you get somewhere. And we're just getting by, just hangin' on... just fitting in... Confident smiles... And we're not very silly, are we, ladies? Noooo. And we don't change our minds or blab our faces off. We don't cry or giggle at the wrong moment, do we? Noooo. And we're really good drivers. And, in the midst of all this mastery of the modern age, along comes little Maggie Trudeau, doodle-doodle-doo... and she falls apart right in the middle of your television set. She says, "I can't cope... I don't know if I'm a wife or a mother, or a career... or which career. I'm silly and narcissistic... I don't... I... A husband...? I don't know... too much... I can't cope! And we don't like that, do we, ladies? Noooo. And we don't like that, do we, gentlemen? Nooooo. Because if Maggie Trudeau, with all the advantages, falls apart, where does that leave us? In the same boat... Welcome aboard. My name is Margaret Trudeau. I'm the woman who gave freedom a bad name. Come on, take a look. I'm not afraid. And I have only one question to ask you... Which do you think is my best feature, my legs... or my bum?

MARGARET *slaps her ass and dances away.*

The music changes and she becomes HENRY.

SCENE NINE

HENRY'S LAST HURRAH

HENRY's first lines are intercut with a sad sixties rock ballad, which fades away as he speaks.

HENRY   I saw Margaret at McDonald's the other day. I was having an Egg McMuffin and a Coke. She was sitting there right as close as you are to me. She didn't recognize me, though, no reason really. She had the kids with her. They're getting so big you'd never recognize them. He came in. He picked up two of the kids, she had the little one; they had an order to go. Then they all went off in the same car. And I thought, here I am trying to conclude my assignment and maybe I never will. Maybe I'm doomed to tell this story over and over again. Was Maggie stupid, nuts? Or just what we needed? Was he the definition of arrogance, did he save the country, did he damn it? I've lost my objectivity, I've completely lost the ability to analyze these people... because I'm so hungry for... something. So seared by something. It's like having been involved in one of those incredible thunderstorms, you know the kind, with the flashes and the crashes and the colours. And you stand there, just a little bit in awe of all that shit on the line up there. And you don't call it good and you don't call it bad, you're thinking of something else. Then after it reaches one of those heights, it starts to die away. You see a little bit of lightning in the distance, and maybe a crash of thunder, maybe a little flash of… something over there… maybe a bit of… that's me. I'm the guy that can't stop watching. But there's a funny thing about those thunderstorms, you can never quite tell when they're over.

The end.

THE DUCHESS
AKA WALLIS SIMPSON

The Duchess: AKA *Wallis Simpson*
is dedicated to
the memory of Clarke Rogers

BEHIND THE BEWITCHING FORCE OF WALLIS SIMPSON: THE KING'S MRS.

Linda Griffiths herself does not realize that I carried her around in my handbag for years. As a young, keen, high-school theatre junkie I stumbled into a used bookstore, and, as always, ran to the theatre section. There on the shelves was the usual fare—Brecht, Shakespeare, Shaw—but a gem of a play entitled *Maggie and Pierre* immediately caught my eye. This was my first taste of Linda Griffiths's daring, unique theatrical style. While the other grade-ten girls revealed *Star Wars* movie-ticket stubs and the latest flavour of lip balm (7UP) from their purses, I proudly pulled out my well-thumbed copy of Griffiths's play with my favourite passages underlined and highlighted, ready for recitation at a moment's notice. That dear play, gently banging in my handbag, accompanied me for the rest of my high-school years, perhaps as a hopeful portrait for my future—strong, interesting, daring women leading unconventional lives. It came as no surprise then that Linda, years later, should write about another strong woman who has fascinated not only me but also the world—the Duchess of Windsor, Wallis Simpson.

Growing up in a British family with an avid royalist for a mother I had seen every film, miniseries, and documentary on Wallis Simpson. There is a predictability and commonality to the treatment of this topic—one starts to recognize the same anecdotes and, indeed, portrayal of the duchess herself—that is, until one experiences Griffiths's explosive play. The first time I read *The Duchess* I don't think I took a breath, except to gasp, infused as it is with such unbridled theatricality, emotional power, wit, and sexual daring.

We begin at the estate auction for the duke and duchess of Windsor, and the master of ceremonies is none other than the very droll and naughty Noël Coward. Griffiths not only allows us to spend an evening with the most notorious woman of our era, but she also brings in one of the most flamboyant, beloved entertainers of our time to titillate us with his wit. The songs and humour of Coward strike a terrific counterpoint to the world of the royal family. And yet, when we meet the royals, once again, Griffiths dares to depict them in a manner never seen on any television miniseries. This is a king that swears and farts and a queen that talks openly about finding a virgin wife for her son: "This Rose must spread her petals for some palace doctor and be certified *hymen intacta*." Griffiths boldly reveals with great humour and surprise a royal family that is real, honest, emotional, and crass. She is not afraid to offend and that unique quality makes for shocking and thrilling theatre. The taboos of Wallis Simpson's sexuality and masculinity have been hinted at in the press and in biographies, but here in this delicious play we get to witness her experiments in one of the best sex scenes I have ever read or had the pleasure of staging. Wallis, with whip in hand and a dominatrix power, leads the future king of England into his first honest, open sexual experience. We are shocked, aroused, and as the opening night audience proved with spontaneous applause, thrilled to celebrate the success of the prince's orgasm.

But Griffiths does not leave all the fun and titillation to the lead characters. She introduces us to a society chorus and personifies the duchess's beloved jewels. We are first introduced to the enticing baubles at the auction house as Ruby, Sapphire, Emerald, and Diamond seduce the audience with their flirtatious manner. We continue to see these jewels as they fashion a magnetic hold over Wallis—a promise of a better, richer, more luxurious life ahead. As Ms. Simpson's journey spirals downward, the jewels don't leave her side but come in and out of the piece in delightful and surprising ways—they serve as the critical voice of England's mob and later as servants in the Bahamas, where they actually break out in a fabulous calypso dance. In Griffiths's world even the jewels have a sense of irony.

It is when we meet the society chorus, however, when we really see Griffiths's talent for dialogue and formidable repartee. Lady Colefax, Lord Falderal, and Count Ribbentrop emerge from a trap door and the sparring begins: "We were celebrating the end of the war. / Which war? / The one with the Nazis. / Oh, that war. Wasn't everybody a Nazi? / No. Just all of your friends." Griffiths's unique vision of the chorus with their arched style brings forth great parody and political satire. But at the heart of all this imagination and spontaneity there is a true portrait of Wallis Simpson.

Wallis as imagined by Griffiths is a real person. She captures her charm, her strength, and her sexuality, but she also succeeds in making her human. It is difficult for us to imagine such a woman, someone who could exert such bewitching force on a man that he would give up a kingdom for her. Somehow Griffiths succeeds in humanizing a woman who had been demonized by an entire nation. She simply places Wallis so deftly in the context of her time that she allows us to see a real woman—strong, ambitious, daring, and vulnerable. A woman capable of showing grace and courage to the end.

As a director, at every turn I was inspired by the freshness and inventiveness of Griffiths's world, one I found to be theatrically inspiring. *The Duchess* sparked my imagination and it was a delight to stage and a joy to infuse with music and dance. This play is a theatrical feast. I now have a new well-read copy of a Linda Griffiths play banging away in my handbag. I can't wait to see what lands in there next.

—Sarah Rodgers

Sarah Rodgers is an acclaimed actor and director based out of Vancouver.

AUTHOR'S NOTES

The mind boggles at the thought of the many things you could say about how to perform *The Duchess*, but there's only one area that might be any help at all to future productions. It concerns the *Canadian commedia* style of it. In the stage directions, I use *commedia dell'arte* as a catch-all, the best term I know to describe an approach to the society chorus. It doesn't fit exactly, but then nothing does, and *commedia* is one of the basic touchstones.

The characters are at their most effective when a balance is found between their comic potential and the reality of their emotions and situation. In the first production, David Fox as the king in "The Death of the King" scene could have had the audience roaring and guffawing at any given moment. It was as if he held the strings to the audience's responses in his hands; while the parody of a recognized British style was real to them, the fact that the king was dying was also real to them. Fox would loosen the strings to the laughter at certain times, as if to let off steam, then rein the audience in again. When Jennifer Phipps as the queen wept at the king's death, her tears were real.

There are humorous scenes with moments of seriousness, and serious scenes that turn on a bit of silliness, and then return—whatever this might be called, different versions and evolutions have been used in Canadian theatre for many years. In this variation, director Paul Thompson and the actors found a way to give depth and subtlety to characters that might otherwise be considered utterly "*commedia*-ish." Act Two of the play takes us into a darker emotional territory than the first, and if this complexity of playing is found at the beginning, the characters make sense later on. But it won't work if no one has any fun.

I would like to thank the Canada Council for the Arts, the Laidlaw Foundation, the National Arts Centre, the Ontario Arts Council, Alberta Theatre Projects, Simon Heath, Mr. and Mrs. P. Griffiths, Susan Serran, and Paul Thompson.

Many extraordinary actors gave their time and talent in the development of this play. Many thanks to Sandra Balcovske, Bob Bainborough, John Blackwood, Greg Kramer, Bev Cooper, Greg Morrison, Jennifer Phipps, Judy Marshak, Karen Hines, Richard McMillan, Jovanni Sy, Steven Morel, Jonathan Wilson, Nancy Beatty, Anne Anglin, Tom Rooney, Kate Newby, Andrew Moodie, Bill Webster, Donna Belleville, Anthony Santiago, and Alex Thompson.

The Duchess: AKA *Wallis Simpson* premiered in Toronto at Theatre Passe Muraille on January 31, 1998, with the following cast and creative team:

Lord Falderal, et al.: David Fox
The Debutante, et al.: Donnna Goodhand
Wallis Simpson: Linda Griffiths
Count Von Ribbentrop, et al.: John Jarvis
Noël Coward, et al.: Louis Negin
Lady Colefax, et al.: Jennifer Phipps
The Prince, et al.: Jonathan Wilson

Director: Paul Thompson
Assistant director: Soheil Parsa
Dramaturgy: Paul Thompson
Stage manager: Kathryn Davies
Apprentice stage manager: Jenny Sinclair
Set and costume design: Astrid Janson
Lighting design: Lesley Wilkinson
Sound design: Rick Sacks

Ladies and gallants of our court, to end
And give a timely period to our sports,
Let us conclude them with declining night;
Our Empire is but of the darker half.

—Ben Jonson, *Cynthia's Revels*

CHARACTERS

Wallis Simpson

The Society Chorus

Noël Coward
Maki
Courtier
Doctor

The Prince
Emerald
Edward, Prince of Wales
(future Edward viii)
Chevy Jones

The Debutante
Patti
Lady Elizabeth (future Queen
Mother)

Lord Falderal
Diamond
Felipe Espil
King George v
Archbishop
Adolf Hitler

Lady Colefax
Sapphire
Shoko
Queen Mary

Count Von Ribbentrop
Bombay Ruby
Win Spencer
Count Ciano
Ernest Simpson
Bertie (future George vi)

ACT ONE
SCENE ONE

THE SOTHEBY AUCTION

Music. Heraldic banners hang from statues of the gods. In the dark we hear the sound of a gavel pounding. Lights up on a bare stage, except for a piano and the auctioneer, NOËL Coward. As he speaks, an opaque black curtain lifts from the scene.

NOËL   Ladies and gentlemen, my name is Noël Coward. Please, no applause. *(elicits applause from audience)* I am here to welcome you to the auction of the century. Tonight, as the shadows lengthen and the lights, carefully placed to flatter aging faces, are turned low, we propose to auction off the entire possessions of the Duchess of Windsor, the infamous Wallis Simpson.

She and the duke lived the love story of the century, a Faerie-tale romance: he the Faerie Prince, she the mortal commoner. Of course, this kind of union usually brings disaster, if not a disastrous sex life — mortal/immortal, you know what I mean... But what you are buying tonight is romance, and if you want to know whether or not they were Nazis, I refer you to seventeen conflicting accounts of every moment of their lives.

I see luminaries from all over the world, prepared to buy pain and a Faerie tale, and for that reason we expect these items to go for fifty to sixty times their value. Yes, you are slavering for these objects now, for whatever power they will bring. For the famous abdication table, a mouldy piece of wedding cake, a few of his used golf balls—how did they get in? But the most spectacular item is lot number one. The fabulous jewels of the Duchess of Windsor.

> *The jewels burst from beneath* NOËL's *feet. They are excited to be suddenly free. They wave glittering hands to the audience, eliciting bids in exotic accents.*

EMERALD   *(East Indian accent)* A flawless emerald ring cut from a stone the size of a bird's egg that once belonged to a Mughal emperor.

RUBY   *(Burmese accent)* A Cartier bracelet set with two exquisite cushion-shaped Burmese rubies.

DIAMOND   *(African accent)* The flamboyant flamingo broach with articulated diamond leg and pavé-set body.

SAPPHIRE	(*Russian accent*) A buckle of cushion-set sapphires surrounded by a sunburst of baguette diamonds.
DIAMOND	The proud head and glittering eyes of an articulated panther bracelet.
NOËL	(*to jewels*) That's enough. / Thank you.
DIAMOND	(*very quickly*) Pear-shaped yellow diamond ear clips.
NOËL	I said, enough.
DIAMOND	The diamond-encrusted heart topped—
NOËL	(*to jewels*) Settle down. I said settle down. Let the bidding begin. And what do I hear for the Mughal emerald?
	Music: "Twentieth Century Blues."
	A crash of thunder. The lights flash. As if torn from a storm, WALLIS *Simpson is catapulted onto the stage, a mad old woman.*
WALLIS	(*to audience member*) Oh no you don't. Bid on that emerald and I'll stab you to death with my hat pin. And if that seems too tame, you haven't seen my hat pin. Yes, it's true, it's all true. It was my fault, the whole century. But that doesn't mean they can

steal my things, rip everything apart, sell to the highest bidder. My jewels, my jewels, my jewels... They want to murder me. This is the second time they've hijacked me. It's the royal family—sending me death threats, sending me bombs...

The jewels are both overjoyed and frightened to see their mistress. They play to the audience in unsubtle ways.

(to jewels) Stop stealing my scene.

The jewels disappear.

I was the Yoko Ono of my generation. Well, the king and I didn't make albums together, but the analogy still holds. I stole a king and made him betray his fans. I know what it is to be reviled. The royals never forgive. But in the end, I won. I climbed and I climbed and I climbed. And when there was nothing, I knew what I would do: I would climb and climb and climb. Where was the top? Kings, of course. Kings are the top, aren't they? Well, aren't they?

NOËL   Wallis?

WALLIS   Noël.

NOËL   I heard you went quite gaga at the end.

WALLIS   I heard you died in the arms of a twelve-year-old
              sailor.

NOËL   Fifteen, he was fifteen. I didn't expect to... conjure
              you up, so to speak.

WALLIS   What did you expect? That my ghost would rest qui-
              etly in its little grave?

NOËL   What do you want?

WALLIS   I want them all to know you can't just get rid of
              women like me. We stick.

NOËL   Go away.

WALLIS   (to audience) Do you want me to go away? Some of
              you do, but some of you don't. Come with me. We'll
              forget the stock-market crash—recession/depression,
              Iraq, Afghanistan, depleted oil stocks, and the whole
              Middle East thing—

NOËL   There's still Hitler.

WALLIS   Everyone's sick of Hitler.

              (to audience) Let's be wicked. We'll have cocktails,
              fabulous hors d'oeuvres, we'll wear glittering jewels,
              beautiful clothes, listen to jazz, laugh ourselves sick,

go dancing, take a yacht—not one of those cruise boats—mausoleums of the middle class—

NOËL   Luring them with luxury is simply cheap.

WALLIS   Once upon a time there was a poor southern girl, with hair as black as ebony, lips as red as blood, skin as white as snow, and a face like a plank.

NOËL   Not quite a plank. I hate to admit it, but you had style.

WALLIS   Fashions fade, style is eternal.

NOËL smiles.

Is that a smirk?

NOËL   Of course it's a smirk. (WALLIS *barks a laugh.*) I've missed that laugh, you witch. I've missed your vulgarity. The Americans invented vulgarity; it's like a dash of paprika in a good dish. There's nothing you can do here, Wallis.

WALLIS   Oh, there's something I can do. I can wake them up.

NOËL   You wouldn't.

WALLIS   *(raising her arms)* I call the society ghosties, the Faeries in hiding, the goblins of my time, to speak!

You tried to destroy me and now you will do my bidding. Get out your corsets, my ghosties, and powder up those lumps. Tie the waistcoats tighter, and smooth out the bumps. Wake up. Wake them all up.

> *There are groans from beneath the stage. A door opens, music and smoke pour out. The* SOCIETY CHORUS *climb into sight, confused and beautiful. They enter a world from which they have been exiled, and return with a hangover. Lord* FALDERAL, *Lady* COLEFAX, *Count Von* RIBBENTROP, *the* DEBUTANTE, *and the* PRINCE *transform into all future characters, yet somehow remain themselves.*

FALDERAL   OHHH, my head…

DEBUTANTE   What is it we were drinking?

RIBBENTROP   We were celebrating the end of the war—

COLEFAX   Which war?

NOËL   The one with the Nazis.

COLEFAX   Oh, that war. Wasn't everybody a Nazi?

NOËL   No, just all of your friends.

RIBBENTROP   No one understands Europe. No one.

FALDERAL   *(sees WALLIS)* Sshh!

COLEFAX   That woman! She caused the war.

DEBUTANTE   That's right. Wallis Simpson caused both world wars.

COLEFAX   And the Depression.

DEBUTANTE   And the Depression. And the decline of family values, and the—

RIBBENTROP   It was obvious there had to be a united Europe, and no one would listen, but Wallis listened, and—

FALDERAL   We should do something beastly. We did, didn't we? We cursed her.

COLEFAX   We cursed her, then she cursed us back.

DEBUTANTE   *(to WALLIS)* You stole our Faerie Prince.

WALLIS   You kicked him out.

NOËL   Now we're all out of the closet, so to speak. It's good to see you again.

WALLIS   Is it?

NOËL   Do you remember the time that we—

WALLIS   No.

NOËL   Perhaps we should explain to the bidders that ref-
              erences to "Faerie" have nothing to do with vulgar
              allusions to homosexuals. Faerie is a place, also a
              state of mind—ancient, deadly, enticing, sexual. A
              place a mortal blunders into on a moonlit night,
              and if escape is possible, finds they've aged a hun-
              dred years. And if a Faerie person ever leaves, they
              lose their magic against death. They're usually rather
              inbred, so the folk are often in search of new blood—

WALLIS   Enough. I'm Faerie Queene now. It's time to remem-
              ber, even if remembering makes you feel alive in
              places you wish were dead. I command you to
              remember.

              *The SOCIETY CHORUS, in fits and starts, begin to
              remember who they were and what they were.*

CHORUS   Once upon a... once upon a time. Once upon
              a time...

PRINCE   *(suddenly)* Once upon a time there was a prince, a
              Faerie Prince, beloved of all the world. A prince of
              hearts, he dined on tarts and danced with mortal
              girls, and then he met—

WALLIS   Not yet.

PRINCE   But… but soon.

WALLIS   Yes, soon.

PRINCE   Darling, I—

WALLIS   Don't love me yet.

NOËL   Keep your shorts on, Prince, we'll get to you. All right. Once upon a time there was a poor girl with oil-drilling eyes and a will of iron.

WALLIS   An innocent young girl—

NOËL   Innocent?

WALLIS   Whose husband drank, and locked her in the bathroom, and took her to China—

NOËL   China's going to be a problem.

WALLIS   What do you mean, "China's going to be a problem?"

NOËL   Well, they've just been jewels, then they turned into the society chorus, now we have to get them to China and turn them into prostitutes—it's just messy.

WALLIS   Do it.

NOËL   We are in your power, oh Queen.

SCENE TWO

CHINA

The sound of gongs. The SOCIETY CHORUS *creates China with pillows of peach satin and kimonos of the deepest hues; banners embroidered with scarlet dragons drop from the gods.*

NOËL   China, 1922. Wallis with Husband Number One. Oh, he was a son of a gun.

A place of prophesy. A land on the verge of revolution, an emperor dying, a dynasty falling. The flower boats of Shanghai, a place for innocence to die. Her navy husband rode the waves and Wallis followed, her marriage to save.

WALLIS becomes young. WIN *Spencer grabs her, swigging from a bottle. It is as if they have been to a party, and* WIN *has dragged her to the flower boats on a dare.*

WALLIS   But where are we going?

WIN   We're going to the best whorehouse in the world.

SHOKO, PATTI, and MAKI are waiting. They are all sensual and learned.

WALLIS   They don't look like whores.

SHOKO   Welcome.

MAKI   Welcome.

PATTI   You are here to learn the mysteries of Fang Chung?

WIN   *(to WALLIS)* These flower-boat gals can make you feel
           like you're the only man in the world, like you're the
           most fascinating, the smartest, the funniest, the most
           virile—and what they can do with the old balls and
           sceptre is unbelievable.

WALLIS   Don't expect me to be shocked. It sounds like fun.

WIN   Shut up. This is my wife, but I don't want a wife, I
           want a whore. Teach her the works. Fang Chung,
           chung chung… then maybe we can all get in the
           sack together and—

SHOKO   *(recognizing WALLIS)* Oh, my goodness.

MAKI   Yes, we will teach her. She is…?

WALLIS   Wallis.

SHOKO   Wallis?

WALLIS   My mother thought I would be a boy, so she called me—

SHOKO   You are very special. We will teach you everything.

WIN   Hey, don't forget me. Don't forget the old "twig and berries."

MAKI   No, not forget.

          They begin to massage WALLIS *in places that surprise her.*

WALLIS   I always thought there was something about the East... something— *(a gasp of pleasure)*

          The sound of gunshots.

WIN   Jesus Christ, that was close.

SHOKO   It's the Revolution. Now, about your wife... *(They pass the opium pipe.)* We have many things to teach her, about power, about knowledge—

WIN   Forget all that stuff. Teach her to make me as horny as a toad, and I'll be happy. Now, why don't we all get on those pretty pillows and—

          Gunfire again, very loud. Bombs. The sound of buildings falling. Distant screams.

	Hey, what's going on here, what are you trying to pull?
MAKI	It is just the empire falling. This is first of three falling empires your wife will see.
WIN	We're getting out of here. This whole place is about to blow.
WALLIS	But I want to learn Fang Chung, whatever it is.
WIN	You think this is a joke? We're going. Now!
SHOKO	*(urgently to WALLIS)* Please stay.
PATTI	Please stay.
MAKI	Please stay.
WIN	You're playing up to them, and they love you, don't they? Your mother was a whore, and you're a whore.
WALLIS	My mother is better than you'll ever be.
WIN	Oh no, I'm not good enough to wipe your skinny little ass. Who's good enough for you? The king of England?
WALLIS	I'm going to get a divorce.

WIN	Divorce me and you'll be stuck without a dime.
WALLIS	I'm stuck without a dime now.
WIN	You'll never look down your nose at me again!

> *He punches* WALLIS *brutally in the stomach. She doubles over.*

You like a man who can control you. You'll be back. You followed me east, and you'll follow me home.

> WIN *staggers off.* WALLIS *falls,* SHOKO *catches her.* WALLIS *writhes on the pillows in pain.*

WALLIS	Oh God. I'm dying… I'm bleeding.
SHOKO	Relax yourself. Breathe deep. The pain will go away.

> *They again begin to massage* WALLIS, *but this time they are imparting something more mysterious.*

WALLIS	Blood everywhere.
SHOKO	You are no longer pregnant.
WALLIS	I was pregnant?
PATTI	We are sorry. There will be no children.

MAKI   There is always a price for knowledge.

PATTI   Knowledge is power.

SHOKO   The power to hold a man from orgasm for a very
                long time.

PATTI   The knowledge of when to speak and when to be still.

WALLIS   I have to go, I have to find Win. He'll be sorry… he'll
                be good to me now…

SHOKO   You will divorce once, divorce twice, and marry again.

PATTI   One day, you will be in a position of great power.

WALLIS   That's right, I'm going to be president.

                They laugh.

PATTI   Good, you are tough. But your power will come
                because of a man. This will be very hard; you will
                want it for yourself.

                Louder guns and shooting.

MAKI   The Revolution. We must hurry.

PATTI   Notice brushing movements of fingers over nerve
                centres of body—

SHOKO   Press firmly here. Very good for premature ejaculation.

MAKI   Can arouse a dead man—

           They laugh.

           More gunfire. Even closer.

           There is not much time.

SHOKO   It is too soon.

PATTI   We have no choice.

WALLIS   What about... the blood?

PATTI   We are sorry. But you will have a life such as few women have ever lived.

           They raise WALLIS *up, chanting and touching her in strange ways. She begins to move sensually, sexually; her body opens and reaches.*

SHOKO   Keep moving, keep breathing, use your mind like a bird, use your mind like a lion...

WALLIS   *(reaching a point of ecstasy)* It... feels... like, like... a... Revolution!

The guns of the Revolution fire in unison. WALLIS *rises, as if created anew. She wears a chic, severe dress. A schoolmarm costumed by Dior.*

SHOKO   The mind and body are one. Speak.

WALLIS   You can never be too rich… or too thin.

          SHOKO, PATTI, *and* MAKI *laugh, and disappear.*

SCENE THREE

THE SUITORS

Music: "Someday I'll Find You." The SOCIETY CHORUS *transforms itself into a trio of eligible men who dance with* WALLIS, *cutting in and competing for her favours. These tuxedoed figures change characters and accents with surgical precision.*

CIANO   Welcome to Washington. I am the handsome, dark, moody, Italian Fascist, Count Ciano.

WALLIS   Pleased to meet you, Count. I'm here to visit my cousin, and I'm quite overwhelmed. Do you think it's Fascism that makes Italian men so sensual?

ESPIL   I am Don Felipe Espil, first secretary to the Argentine embassy. I dance the best tango in town. I have

                    powerful family connections with President Irigoyen,
                    who suppresses unions.

WALLIS   Tell me more. About the president, about the unions,
                    and the tango.

JONES   I'm Chevy Jones. I represent reality. There's a depres-
                    sion going on, we're fighting for unions and a fair
                    deal for the worker. I play the harmonica and like
                    to make long speeches about left-wing politics.

RIBBENTROP Count Von Ribbentrop at your service. At one time,
                    I was a socialist.

WALLIS   Charming.

RIBBENTROP Now, I'm a National Socialist.

ESPIL   Hitler sends him round to infiltrate society.

WALLIS   He can infiltrate me any time he wants.

                    Everyone laughs.

RIBBENTROP Wallis, there is no one I would rather dance with,
                    but my führer needs me. May we meet again
                    some day.

CIANO   Wallis, you are the most exciting woman in the world,
                    but I must go.

ESPIL   Wallis, I yearn to dance the tango with you again,
            but I must go.

WALLIS   Now wait a cotton-pickin' minute. Not one of you
            is going to marry me? Not rich enough? Not pretty
            enough? Look, one of you has got to take me, the
            money is running out.

ERNEST   Ernest Simpson. I'm a slightly pretentious anglophile
            with a fake British accent and a love for antique china. I
            have a fairly prosperous London-based import business,
            a certain amount of class, and I'm a steady, genuine, if
            slightly dull, human being. May I join the dance?

WALLIS   Are you offering me a certain amount of security, a
            chance to live abroad, and companionship, but no
            exciting dips and dives?

ERNEST   Correct. I also love you.

WALLIS   Felipe, save me.

ESPIL   I am sorry. Good bye, my little Baltimore oriole.

ERNEST   Wallis, will you marry me?

WALLIS   Yes.

SCENE FOUR

WALLIS

> WALLIS *turns to the audience. She is chatty, reasonable, and fun.*

WALLIS   I know what you're thinking. She's just after a meal ticket. That's how it was then, and maybe that's how it is still. I worked. It's hard work to be the belle of the ball. But then, you can go quiet all of a sudden and listen to the men talk about power. You can watch how their minds, and other things… grow to take on the theories of the world. The theories were what made me wet. And as for the magic, it was right down there, you know where I mean? You don't? How terrible for you. You need some pep.

> WALLIS *picks out a perfect subject in the audience.*

Especially you. Now you and I both know you shouldn't have worn that tonight, don't we? You were in a hurry and you just threw it together. Never do that. Beauty you have to be born with, money is hard to find, but style anybody can have. It's hard work. You see, it was so frustrating. All that power and no place to put it. Sound familiar?

SCENE FIVE

BOREDOM

> *A ticking clock.* WALLIS *and* ERNEST *are sitting in their apartment.* WALLIS *is knitting a golden sweater. From somewhere outside we hear the sound of tinkling glasses, chatter, and laughter.*

ERNEST   This is nice, dear, isn't it?

WALLIS   Very nice, dear.

ERNEST   Just you and me by the fire, me with my papers and you with your—

WALLIS   Knitting! Sorry, darling.

ERNEST   A bit glum?

WALLIS   Just a bit. I can hear something outside.

ERNEST   What?

WALLIS   Nothing, just… I can't believe this is what they meant.

ERNEST   What?

WALLIS   Oh, I had my fortune told in China and they said I was going to be rich and famous. I'm so restless, I can't keep still.

ERNEST   I'm just happy to hear the sounds of the Old World.

WALLIS   Old. Ancient. I love how old the buildings are, everything's solid. And I hate how old the buildings are, everything's stolid. Something's going to happen, I can feel it.

ERNEST   What?

WALLIS   Ernest, help me. I want to be good. I want to stay here, with you, by the fire, but...

ERNEST   But what?

WALLIS   Don't let me do it.

ERNEST   Do what?

WALLIS   Do whatever it is I'm going to do.

ERNEST   My dear, calm yourself, you're delirious.

WALLIS   Just one invitation. That's all I need, one invitation to the right place at the right time with the right people.

ERNEST Well, if it's invitations you want, my sister should be able to manage something. She knows Dame Sibyl Colefax. Will that do? Now come and sit down quietly.

WALLIS I can't. I want to climb up these walls, crawl out the window, leap into the street, and run forever.

Music: "Mad Dogs and Englishmen."

SCENE SIX

CROWNS

Buckingham Palace, 1933. KING *George* V; EDWARD, *Prince of Wales; and his mother,* QUEEN *Mary.* EDWARD *quickly stubs out a cigarette.*

KING You were late again for an appointment with the Agricultural Society, and then you arrive in plus fours. You act like a cad, you dress like a cad, you are a cad!

EDWARD *(fighting back tears)* Sir, I—

QUEEN Listen to your father, David.

KING You are a loose cannon. You are outspoken about vague liberal politics which you barely understand, you don't go to church, you spend your nights at the Embassy Club—

EDWARD My ideas are not vague and not particularly liberal. We have lost touch with the people. They need housing and hospitals, they need—

KING Balderdash. What you really want to do is gad about.

EDWARD I am a salesman for the empire! I have travelled to Africa, India, South America, Australia, New

Zealand, Canada… I have clocked in one hundred thousand miles for the empire.

KING   And what could have possibly possessed you to buy a cattle ranch in Alberta, Canada?

QUEEN   You were reported to be in a highly nervous state, smoking constantly and drinking whiskey at all hours.

EDWARD   It was very beautiful—the farm, I mean, not the whiskey.

QUEEN   Don't be impertinent.

KING   I hear you are more popular than Rudolph Valentino. If you wear a sweater with a bloody scarf, half the world copies it! And this business of shaking hands with the people, losing the vital distance of monarchy by touching them. They scream and mob you like some dancer from the continent. But you seem to find the ceremony and ritual of kingship, not to mention the duties, distasteful.

EDWARD   There are times when I am… very bored, sir.

KING   Bored! He gets bored! Monarchies are falling all over Europe, and he's bored!

QUEEN   The czar was shot, your uncle was shot, they're shooting monarchs all over the place these days. We are walking on a precipice.

KING   Do you want to become king? Do you?

EDWARD   What do you expect me to answer?

KING   I expect you to answer yes! I expect you to marry and
              produce heirs! I expect you—go and bring me that box.

              *EDWARD sees a plain wooden box and brings it to
              his father. The KING places it on his lap and opens
              it. Shining inside is the royal crown.*

EDWARD   Is it the real thing or just another copy?

KING   You can't tell the real thing when you see it? The
              golden orb, representing the sun. The king is like the
              sun, giving warmth and prosperity to his people. This
              may seem like an outmoded, even mystical concept,
              but I assure you, it has a great deal of power. If the
              king fails, the country fails. I am going to offer you
              this crown. You must accept it, with all its attendant
              responsibilities, into your very soul.

              *He holds out the crown to EDWARD. A long silence.
              EDWARD takes the crown. He weeps.*

QUEEN   We let you have too much freedom, David. It's
              not entirely your fault that you are terminally
              high-strung.

              The QUEEN leaves the room.

KING   My father was afraid of his father, I was afraid of my
         father, and I've made damn sure that you are terrified
         of me. You do understand, don't you, David?

EDWARD   Yes.

SCENE SEVEN

THE BALL

> *The music is an eerie waltz.* WALLIS *and* ERNEST,
> *dressed to the nines, stand in front of a wall of
> shimmering curtains. Behind the wall we the
> hear the sound of Lady* COLEFAX's *salon, catch a
> glimpse of the* SOCIETY CHORUS *dancing with dress-
> maker's dummies clad in the latest elegance. Lord*
> FALDERAL, *Lady* COLEFAX, *the* DEBUTANTE, *Count
> Von* RIBBENTROP, *and* NOËL *Coward.*

ERNEST   My dear, I've never seen you so… unnerved.

WALLIS   Unnerved? I'm ready to pee my pants.

ERNEST   You must knock.

WALLIS   My dress makes me look fat, my accent is totally
         wrong—

ERNEST   None of that matters. You're American, you have that
            gift of easy friendliness. Very rare here.

WALLIS   Ernest, you are a sweet, sweet man.

            They kiss lightly.

ERNEST   And you are a bubble that will rise to its own level.

            *WALLIS knocks. The dancers freeze briefly, then
            continue.*

FALDERAL   Who is that?

COLEFAX   Who's there?

ERNEST   Wallis and Ernest Simpson.

COLEFAX   Do we know them?

NOËL   You can't just come in like that. You have to know
            the password.

WALLIS   Is it money?

COLEFAX   How crass. Close the door.

WALLIS   No. Is it prestige?

FALDERAL   Prestige is boring.

WALLIS   What about cocktails?

COLEFAX   Cocktails?

WALLIS   I know how to make cocktails that will have you
                hallucinating your wildest thoughts, your dearest
                dreams, your most—

COLEFAX   I haven't had a wild thought in years, if indeed, ever.

NOËL   New blood.

DEBUTANTE   New blood?

COLEFAX   Let them in.

NOËL   *(to WALLIS)* Are you certain you want to enter these
                gates?

WALLIS   I am.

NOËL   What about the price?

WALLIS   You don't think there's a price to being on the out-
                side? Let me in.

NOËL   Enter at your own risk. Look, but touch nothing. Eat
                nothing, drink nothing, or you might be caught for-
                ever. They would cut off your breasts and feed them
                to you for breakfast, à la florentine.

He opens the curtains. A cloud of Faerie dust as WALLIS *enters the kingdom. Music. A burst of laughter.* WALLIS *stares at the glory of it all.*

COLEFAX   We are golden, we are lace…

DEBUTANTE We are wit, we are grace…

FALDERAL   Some might say we are a "Master Race."

RIBBENTROP "A master race…"

NOËL   I am but the doorman to this Faerie Land. Tolerated mostly, with a smile. But one false move and it's no more Mr. Coward, this doorman goes the way of Oscar Wilde.

WALLIS   False humility. You are the most famous playwright in Britain. Be a doll and do the introductions.

FALDERAL   I think she should guess.

COLEFAX   Perhaps we should blindfold her, that would be fun.

WALLIS   Go ahead, I can be a sport.

> NOËL *produces a blindfold that resembles a piece of lingerie.*

DEBUTANTE No peeking. *(spinning* WALLIS*)* One…

COLEFAX   Two. Three!

WALLIS   *(feels her way around the room)* I smell someone
              very… manly and powerful, with investments in
              every pie in Europe. *(finds Lord FALDERAL)* And his
              name is Lord Falderal.

FALDERAL   How did you know?

WALLIS   I'm secretly clairvoyant.

DEBUTANTE   And she reads the Court Circular.

FALDERAL   She makes me feel that I'm the most fascinating man,
              the most charming, the most virile—

WALLIS   Now, let me see… Here is the debutante of the
              season, Sylvia Chalksworth. She appears shy and
              sweet, but underneath those big cotton panties, she's
              a bomb ready to go off.

              Delighted laughter from the CHORUS.

DEBUTANTE   I am, I really am!

WALLIS   And you must be… Lady Colefax, Society Queen of
              London. Your corsets are always made of blue satin and
              you haven't slept with your husband in twenty years.

COLEFAX   Thirty.

WALLIS   I already know Count Von Ribbentrop, the most
              stylish Fascist in town.

              ELIZABETH enters.

              Oh, oh, oh, oh, and you must be the prince's sister-
              in-law, the smiling Duchess of York. I wonder if your
              smile is as warm as they say—maybe you're just a few
              gems short of a tiara. But for the moment I'll buy
              that genteel grin, and hope I get to test it… over a
              big glass of gin!

              *She pulls off her blindfold with a flourish.
              Applause from the CHORUS.*

              Everyone, this is my husband, Ernest.

NOËL   It's very important to be Ernest.

WALLIS   Lady Colefax, I'm going to be very forward and ask
              you a big favour.

COLEFAX   Go ahead, my dear. *(sotto voce)* We love your vivacity,
              but your need to enter is a little obvious. You must
              learn to tone yourself down if you want to get on in
              London society.

WALLIS   Thanks, I'll work on it. Now, do you have a record
              player? Ernest? Have you got it? This is my favourite

music from the States. There's a dance that goes with it, called "The Black Bottom."

COLEFAX   The black what?

NOËL   I believe she said "bottom," ma'am.

DEBUTANTE   Wallis, you're so exciting, you make me feel like I am exciting, and fascinating, and interesting—

WALLIS   Now, I'm going to teach you all this dance. But first of all, we need cocktails. Noël, don't be so stuffy, I know you've heard of cocktails.

NOËL   I've heard rumours.

Von RIBBENTROP hands WALLIS a tray of cocktail glasses.

RIBBENTROP   Mrs. Simpson, your husband asked me to assist you.

WALLIS   Count, always so helpful.

RIBBENTROP   At your service.

WALLIS drops a secret potion in the glasses and they begin to smoke and bubble. The CHORUS eagerly grab their cocktails.

WALLIS   All the zest of New York City in one deadly glass.

ELIZABETH *(refusing a glass)* No, thank you.

WALLIS Suit yourself.

ELIZABETH This is the kind of gathering where people talk, exchange views.

WALLIS Oh. I just thought it was time for a little fun.

ELIZABETH There are many different kinds of "fun."

WALLIS Really? I only know one kind. The kind where you feel like a champagne bottle that's just been uncorked. Like all your bubbles are bursting.

> *Music: "The Black Bottom."*

Now stand back and let me see if I've got this right.

> WALLIS *does some steps, which include holding, slapping, and spanking her bottom. In rhythm, of course. The* CHORUS *follow. Enter* EDWARD, *Prince of Wales. He stands behind the crowd, unseen.*

You may look a little silly to start off with, but don't worry, it's a wise man who knows he's a fool. Think of your brains and your body as being the same thing.

COLEFAX Ridiculous. My mind and body have never even met.

FALDERAL   Like this?

WALLIS   Yes! You've got it!

            Finally, WALLIS notices the newcomer.

            Now there's someone new here, we're going to have
            to initiate him.

COLEFAX   Oh, my God, His Royal Highness.

            She sinks into a curtsy.

EDWARD   Please, no formality.

WALLIS   His Royal—? Oh, oh, I… I'm so…

            She is so nervous her words come out in gibberish.

            I dglophscneg… I don't even know how to curtsy.

EDWARD   That was really very good. I see you're American.

WALLIS   That's right, sir. A crass, ambitious American trying
            to make her way through the complexities of British
            society.

EDWARD   And how are you doing?

WALLIS   Pretty well. And you?

EDWARD   Oh, I have the complexities of British society running through my blood.

WALLIS   And where else?

EDWARD   I'm sorry, I…

WALLIS   I'm disappointed. I thought the complexities of British society were situated in the prince's staff of power, so to speak.

FALDERAL   Staff of power… can she possibly mean… Oh, my God!

NOËL   Oh, she means it. Brilliant. She brings a man's mind right down to where his brains are located.

EDWARD   Actually, it's in the crown jewels, so to speak.

            EDWARD and WALLIS *laugh.*

ELIZABETH   *(to* FALDERAL*)* I think you should save him.

COLEFAX   Mrs. Simpson? Why don't you—

            EDWARD *is about to light a cigarette when* WALLIS *slaps his hand.*

WALLIS   Naughty. That's such a rotten habit, you really have to quit.

The SOCIÉTY CHORUS *gasps.*

COLEFAX   She slapped his hand, and he's not supposed to even be touched!

EDWARD   You're quite right, it is naughty.

          NOËL *Coward and Lord* FALDERAL *capture* EDWARD.

NOËL   Your Royal Highness…

FALDERAL   Your Highness, have you heard the one about the two dancers…?

ELIZABETH   Play the waltz.

          The slow eerie waltz starts up again.

WALLIS   Why have they changed the music?

RIBBENTROP   Mrs. Simpson, what a pleasure to see you again. I hope to drop by on you and your husband very soon.

WALLIS   Yes, Count von Ribbentrop, that would be swell, but why have they—

EDWARD   "Swell?" How lovely. Mrs. Simpson?

WALLIS   Yes, Your Highness?

EDWARD   That music you played, is it by any chance "The Black Bottom"?

WALLIS   You know it?

EDWARD   Does that surprise you? I think Fred Astaire taught me—

WALLIS   Fred Astaire? You know Fred—

EDWARD   He stole the cut of his tuxedo from me. But I forgave him. Shall we dance?

           EDWARD snaps his fingers. Instantly "The Black Bottom" plays again.

COLEFAX   Well, I—

ELIZABETH David, I don't think you should be behaving this way—

EDWARD   *(throwing her his jacket)* Elizabeth, don't think for the moment—boogie instead.

           The music intensifies. The SOCIETY CHORUS *join in, except for* ELIZABETH. EDWARD *shows* WALLIS *a new move.*

WALLIS   Oh, that's swell. I didn't know that one.

EDWARD   Then there's this.

           Another step; she copies it.

WALLIS   Don't they call you the Faerie Prince?

EDWARD   I'm completely mortal, as you see.

WALLIS   I'm not sure about that.

EDWARD   You're not afraid of me.

WALLIS   Oh, yes I am.

EDWARD   But it's a different kind of fear—

WALLIS   It's because I'm from another world.

EDWARD   I love the Americas, I love Americans...

           The music hits a peak. The SOCIETY CHORUS *is
           dancing the Black Bottom with perfection.*

WALLIS   The New World!

EDWARD   The New World!

WALLIS   I want to wake you up. I want to shake you up. I want
           the stuff that stuffs your shirts!

EDWARD   Wake me up. Please. Wake me up!

The music hits a crescendo, then stops dead as
WALLIS *and* EDWARD *freeze, looking into each other's eyes.*

SCENE EIGHT

WALLIS

WALLIS *and the audience.*

WALLIS   Wasn't I good? Frankly, I didn't think it would go
that well. I have to have him. Is that wrong? Is it
wrong because I'm married? Is it wrong because I'm
divorced? Divorce, a word like toads coming out of
your mouth. Leper, whore. Breaker of promises.

Now, there is a nasty rumour going around that I
was a man. Oh, I wish. It's true that every once in
a while I would take the cardboard tube from a roll
of toilet paper and tape it between my legs so it…
dangled. It seems a cruel joke God played on you
men to put so many tender objects right out there
in the open. I bet you want to know why I would do
such a thing. Because being a woman wasn't nearly
enough for what I had in mind. And then, I would
take off my cardboard cock and become a woman
again, as much of a woman as any ancient statue…

He's coming, can you feel him? Those huge child eyes, begging me to give him… something. And I couldn't. So I bewitched him instead.

SCENE NINE

THE BEDROOM

A saxophone plays smooth jazz. Blackout. In the darkness we hear squeaking bedsprings, heavy breathing, then silence. Lights up.

EDWARD   I'm sorry, Wallis. Better luck next time.

WALLIS   Talk to me.

EDWARD   About what?

WALLIS   This.

EDWARD   Oh. Well, I… better luck next time. And so on.

WALLIS   Your Highness, Americans aren't so stuffy about these things.

EDWARD   Please call me David, all those close to me do. The world thinks of me as a great lover, but the truth is, I'm not.

WALLIS   Please don't think I'm too forward, sir. David. But I
            learned a few things when I was in China.

EDWARD   The real truth is, I've rarely... actually... fully... done
            it. Well, once or twice.

WALLIS   Premature ejaculation?

EDWARD   I seem to be highly excitable—

WALLIS   Sir. David. Have you ever heard of the art of Fang
            Chung?

EDWARD   Fang...?

WALLIS   Chung. It's a skill, practised for centuries, which
            involves, among other things...

            WALLIS straddles EDWARD and begins to touch him.

            ...relaxation of the male partner through a pro-
            longed and carefully modulated massage of the
            nipples...

EDWARD   Yes...?

WALLIS   The stomach...

EDWARD   Ohhhh, yes...

WALLIS   The thighs... and after a deliberately protracted and titillatingly unbearable delay...

EDWARD   Yes...?

WALLIS   The genitals.

EDWARD   *(breathing heavily)* I've always liked the Chinese.

WALLIS   Do you like to play games?

EDWARD   Games?

WALLIS   *(taking off her long black gloves)* Sometimes when we're intimate, we like to feel big and powerful, sometimes small and... dominated.

EDWARD   I remember my nursery... Mamma was the queen... never there at all, really, and my nanny would...

WALLIS   Trust me.

EDWARD   She would... she would pinch me and spank me... and—

WALLIS   Spank you... like this?

       She whips EDWARD *with her gloves.*

EDWARD   Oh yes, don't stop.

WALLIS   She'd say you were bad.

EDWARD   Yes…

WALLIS   A naughty boy! A bad, naughty, dirty boy!

EDWARD   Yes!

WALLIS   Say "I'm not a bad boy."

EDWARD   I'm not… a bad… I'm not bad…

WALLIS   Say, "I'm the King of England, and I can do as I like!"

EDWARD   I'm not king yet, you know, I'm only Prince of—

WALLIS   Say it.

EDWARD   I'm the King of England and I can do as I like!

WALLIS   Louder!

EDWARD   I'm the King of England, and I can do as I like!

WALLIS   Again!

EDWARD   I'm the King of England… I'm the King of England… I'm the King of England… and I… can… do… as… I… like!

He climaxes.

WALLIS   Just this once, you might want a cigarette. *(lights a cigarette for him)* But in return, you have to tell me about your work.

EDWARD   My work? You're the first woman I've ever met who was interested in my work.

WALLIS   Oh there's nothing better than pillow-talk politics. What do you think of the communists?

EDWARD   I think they're a bunch of lying vipers.

WALLIS   So do I. And what about Europe? Is it possible for there to be peace? Do you think women are secretly more lethal than men could ever be? Will there always be rich and poor, and it doesn't matter what anyone does? Where is the power? Do you have power?

EDWARD   Will the workers always be exploited? Why are they saying God is dead? Do you believe in God?

WALLIS   No, do you?

EDWARD   I think yes.

WALLIS   Sometimes I think of Europe as this great dark rock, and every few years someone raises up the rock, and worms crawl out and begin to feed on each other.

EDWARD   Yes! That's what it's like—only this time it won't happen. And do you know why?

WALLIS   Why?

EDWARD   National Socialism.

WALLIS   Yes!

EDWARD   You know of it?

WALLIS   It's all anyone is talking about in Washington.

EDWARD   The most exciting social experiment of this century. Hitler is a great man. He's brought his people from desperation to prosperity with the speed of lightning.

WALLIS   He has. And what will you do when you're king, and in charge of all those areas of the map coloured pink?

EDWARD   I will be the first modern king. The first to pilot an airplane, to dance to jazz, to speak without that plumby accent, the first to visit ordinary people in their homes. I want to… to loosen the buttons of the monarchy. I am very concerned about housing for the poor.

WALLIS   I know about the poor. I used to be one of them.

EDWARD   We ignore the gulf between rich and poor at our peril.

WALLIS   So the rich must give up a little.

EDWARD   I want to do something with my life and with my reign. I want to have the power to…

WALLIS   The power to…

EDWARD   The power to… there's so much. Would it be considered unmanly if I asked to put my head in your lap?

WALLIS   My lap is here for you anytime.

> EDWARD *lays his head in* WALLIS's *lap. She strokes his golden hair.*

EDWARD   Don't go away.

WALLIS   Shhhh, shhhhh, shhhhhh… there there.

EDWARD   I've been so alone.

WALLIS   There there, my little one, my little boy, there there.

SCENE TEN

THE FIRM

Music: "God Save the King." WALLIS and EDWARD remain on the bed. The royal family enters: the KING, the QUEEN, BERTIE, ELIZABETH, and a COURTIER (NOËL Coward). They do not see the couple on the bed, but perhaps they sense them.

KING   I am the King of Britain, and I can't receive a divorced harlot called Mrs. Simpson.

COURTIER   We think she's a Fascist spy. In this dossier you'll see—

ELIZABETH   Of course, she'd be a spy as well.

COURTIER   There's something about the art of "Fang Chung."

ELIZABETH   Fang Chung?

KING   I hate the sight of him. I've always hated the sight of him.

QUEEN   Lower your voice.

COURTIER   Here is our "China dossier." She spent time in the brothels of China, working as a prostitute. As far as we can tell, she was born illegitimately, but then her parents did finally legalize—

ELIZABETH   But what is Fang Chung?

BERTIE   (*slight stammer*) He can't possibly mean to m-m-marry her.

KING   Speak up, Bertie, for God's sake. Of course he can't bloody marry her. But it's time for him to marry bloody someone!

COURTIER   To some he says he must marry her, to others he insists he has no such intention.

BERTIE   He m-must give her up; if he d-doesn't, there c-could be chaos. You know I have no d-desire to be k-king, g-giving speeches, meeting all those people—

ELIZABETH   We must speak with David, make him see reason before he—

QUEEN   David will frighten us, but he's not a complete fool. The moment will come when he realizes the constitutional advantages of a virgin, and he will find himself an intact English Rose. And while we no longer ride through the streets with the bloody sheets on royal wedding nights, this Rose must spread her petals for a palace doctor and be certified *hymen intacta*. Once she is pried open by the golden sceptre—forgive me if the metaphor is a little obvious—she will be thrown onto a balcony with a crown on her head, to wave to the crowds, and produce as many sons as humanly possible. He will have mistresses, she will survive, and the House of Windsor will rule Britain forever more.

ALL   Amen.

KING   What do you mean, "spread her petals"?

ELIZABETH   I would like to know about this Fang—

QUEEN   That's enough.

COURTIER   Also, there have been some information leaks from the government dispatches. We think she is passing on information learned from the prince, to the Germans.

KING   Will you stop!

ELIZABETH   She's a wicked woman. She has no sense of duty, no finer feelings, no dignity, no education, no honour, no sensitivity, no respect, no—

BERTIE   No b-bum. She really doesn't have much of a bum.

QUEEN   I don't want you to mention that woman's name again.

ELIZABETH   But we must talk about this, decide what to do.

QUEEN   In this family, we regard frank discussion with the same revulsion with which we regard farting in public.

ELIZABETH   By not speaking about it, don't you see we are playing into Mrs. Simpson's hands?

COURTIER   We believe she had an abortion in China that caused her severe gynecological problems—

KING   SHUT UP!! My God, what will happen when I die? He'll make a bollocks of it within a year.

ELIZABETH   But what if David—

QUEEN   He won't. It's unthinkable.

               The QUEEN, KING, and COURTIER leave the scene.

BERTIE   T-time for b-bed, my dear?

ELIZABETH   Bed? Bertie, have you ever liked to play games?

BERTIE   I'm not much for g-games, but I do enjoy tennis.

ELIZABETH   That's not quite what I meant, I meant—

BERTIE   Oh. I'm sorry. I—

ELIZABETH   No, I'm sorry, I—

ELIZABETH puts her finger on BERTIE*'s mouth.*

BERTIE   He's very l-lovable, isn't he? David. People just love him. And he dresses so well, he charms—

ELIZABETH   Charm without grace.

BERTIE   Come, darling, let's look in on the girls. Lillibet is so big now, I hardly know her.

ELIZABETH   After the Great War, the world went into a frenzy. A sort of forced gaiety. Everything became louder, the music, the people. Bad women are in fashion, they are wicked and fun. But in the end, they'll realize that a good woman with a blessed smile is the only thing worth looking up to. Wallis Simpson doesn't know that. She wants to rock the boat and get into it at the same time. We won't let her. Will we, Bertie?

BERTIE   No, we won't, my sweetheart.

SCENE ELEVEN

FEYDEAU

Music: "I've Danced with a Man, Who's Danced with a Girl, Who's Danced with the Prince of Wales." WALLIS *and* ERNEST's *apartment.* WALLIS *enters, madly addressing envelopes and checking lists of guests.* NOËL *Coward watches, amused.*

NOËL   The maid says the invitations cannot wait any longer.

WALLIS   I'm learning as fast as I can. How to arrange a room, how to have a dinner party, how to dress on no money. I've started cocktail hour—it's revolutionary to them, a casual time in a casual home, they love it. Clothes, I need clothes. And shoes, and a day dress—

NOËL   You need to do some thinking.

WALLIS   Thinking? I don't like thinking.

NOËL   It's one thing to get the prince into bed, it's one thing to get inside the gates. Many mortals have dipped their toes in the Faerie stream, but can you live at this altitude, Wallis? I wasn't exactly born to it either, and now I'm better at it than they are.

WALLIS   Are you suggesting we're alike?

NOËL   Good God, no. I'm much more intelligent.

WALLIS   I'm intelligent—sort of.

NOËL   Your intelligence is connected to passion, and therefore unreliable. Now, let's get down to the dirt. There's a rumour going around that you're actually a man.

WALLIS   Funny, there's a rumour going around that you're actually a man.

NOËL   I went swimming with the prince once, and he had the smallest pecker I've ever seen.

WALLIS   I love homosexual men.

NOËL   Yes, you do. Now, isn't that strange? And what about the prince? How gay is he?

WALLIS   Let's leave that one dangling, so to speak.

NOËL   What I really want to know is, do you love him? If you don't, it's more delicious. Consider me a scientist of love. All my plays are about love, especially married people in love.

WALLIS   (disturbed) I don't know what you're talking about. He needs me, he calls me ten times a day, he falls to pieces if we're parted for the weekend, sometimes…

often, I want to run away. Is that what you want to hear? I'm very fond of—

NOËL   Stop. You're frightening me. In spite of my habitual levity, I love this country and you don't. You can't feel it.

WALLIS   You can feel a hand, or tongue; you can feel sad, or even bad, but you can't feel a country.

NOËL   If I could love a woman, it would be you.

He kisses her, then backs away, shocked at himself.

Someone important should come in the door right now, someone challenging, significant, someone… "Fruity."

Lord FALDERAL enters.

FALDERAL   I just couldn't stay away. What a wonderful idea, cocktails!

Count Von RIBBENTROP and the DEBUTANTE enter.

NOËL   Count Von Ribbentrop. And the lovely—

RIBBENTROP   Mrs. Simpson, I can feel the force of your personality through the walls. Mr. Coward.

NOËL   Count.

RIBBENTROP Wallis, I have found you were right. Britain has not even begun to update her armaments. There are no bombers at all and the fighter planes are very few.

NOËL When did you two have that conversation? Wallis, you shouldn't—

WALLIS Oh, don't be silly. We were all talking about bombers and death at Emerald's dinner party. Bombers with the hors d'oeuvres, and death with dessert and coffee.

NOËL And you just thought you'd pass it on?

DEBUTANTE *(seeing the PRINCE)* The Prince of Wales.

EDWARD enters.

EDWARD Wallis! What a dreadful day, I had to see you. I'm just come from the Admiralty. They are going to impose sanctions on Italy, and if they do—

RIBBENTROP Sanctions on Italy? When?

EDWARD Wallis, tell me you agree. There is madness everywhere.

WALLIS Believe in yourself. Don't be afraid of them, remember who you are.

RIBBENTROP Absolutely, there should be no sanctions.

EDWARD   *(to WALLIS)* With you I am never afraid.

NOËL   Sir, perhaps you could… Sir, perhaps be a little more
              discreet, sir?

RIBBENTROP   I must go. Duty calls. Your Highness, Wallis, Mr.
              Coward.

              RIBBENTROP exits.

NOËL   Sir, he is dangerous.

EDWARD   Some people think anyone who believes in peace is
              a pansy.

NOËL   I find that remark—

WALLIS   I find politics madly thrilling.

NOËL   Good. No thinking required for that.

EDWARD   Perhaps you should become prime minister.

NOËL   And what would she be like, I wonder.

WALLIS   She'd be horrible.

EDWARD   By God, I intend my views to influence British policy,
              and soon.

NOËL   That's what they're all afraid of.

WALLIS and the DEBUTANTE *move to a corner.*

DEBUTANTE The men are talking politics again and leaving us
          alone. So boring.

WALLIS   Never say that!

DEBUTANTE You don't see us talking rot.

WALLIS   Exactly. And look where we are.

DEBUTANTE Where are we?

WALLIS   You're a silly girl, and you'll marry a silly man, and
          you'll have silly, unteachable children—

DEBUTANTE I don't appreciate your tone, Wallis.

WALLIS   The dinner ends. The women leave to talk about
          birth, personalities, and love, the men talk about
          politics and economics. We have to get in there with
          both feet—

DEBUTANTE But it's boring.

WALLIS   Keep in the conversation. Don't let them own it. You
          can own it. All you need is a few little phrases.

DEBUTANTE But I don't want to.

WALLIS   Look. Where are the men?

           The DEBUTANTE *looks to see the men huddled across the room.*

DEBUTANTE What phrases?

WALLIS   The Republicans, sorry, the Conservative Party needs to establish where it stands.

DEBUTANTE The Conservative Party—

WALLIS   A strong dollar means a strong world economy.

DEBUTANTE A strong pound—

WALLIS   Oh yes, pound. And of course, Hitler is a great man.

DEBUTANTE I have a little crush on Hitler, that little moustache—

WALLIS   Power is an aphrodisiac.

DEBUTANTE Power is—

WALLIS   Don't repeat it, just think it.

EDWARD   What are you girls talking about?

DEBUTANTE Politics.

WALLIS Power.

FALDERAL You'll never catch a man that way.

DEBUTANTE A strong pound means a strong economy.

FALDERAL Exactly. A strong pound means strong trade.

DEBUTANTE Hitler is a great man.

FALDERAL *(to DEBUTANTE)* You're a smart little thing, aren't you?

DEBUTANTE Just interested.

NOËL *(to WALLIS)* You've created a monster.

FALDERAL Hitler is the antidote to communism.

NOËL What can be expected of the ruling classes is not treachery or physical cowardice, but stupidity.

EDWARD Wallis, what do you think?

WALLIS Hitler's *third way* is more practical than anything else. It's not rampant capitalism and it's certainly not communism.

EDWARD Hear hear.

NOËL   The third way?

FALDERAL   A hybrid of corporatism and social initiatives.

EDWARD   A détente between left and right.

WALLIS   The corporate state.

DEBUTANTE   Wallis, you are a queen.

WALLIS   Not yet.

            ERNEST Simpson enters with a briefcase looking tired.

ERNEST   Your Highness. Noël. *(aside to WALLIS)* Wallis, I'm exhausted, the business is draining me dry, I just want a quiet evening.

WALLIS   Yes, dear, I know it must be horrible for you.

FALDERAL   *(to ERNEST)* What a wonderful idea, old boy. Cocktails every night, just drop in—

            EDWARD pours ERNEST a cocktail.

ERNEST   *(to WALLIS)* Every night. You invited people every night?

WALLIS   Don't be angry, Ernie, it's just for a couple of hours.

ERNEST   I want a quiet—

WALLIS   *(off to invisible French maid)* Estelle? There'll be
             several more for dinner. We must add Chicken
             Maryland as an entree.

EDWARD   Hang dinner, let's go dancing.

ERNEST   Dancing!

NOËL   Ambrose is playing at the Embassy.

WALLIS   *(to ERNEST)* I know you're tired, dear, but His Highness
             wants to go dancing.

EDWARD   Come on, old boy. We need you.

ERNEST   *(to FALDERAL)* He needs me as damned camouflage.

DEBUTANTE Let's go.

FALDERAL   I can't wait. Turn up the music.

             They dance.

EDWARD   I'm getting my own coat!

ERNEST   *(to WALLIS)* I want my home back.

EDWARD   Wally, I'm waiting.

ERNEST   Sir, it's a great honour that you spend so much time with Wallis and... myself, but—

WALLIS   Ernest, please! David, I know you're used to getting your way, but you must learn to be more aware of people's feelings.

EDWARD   Yes, Wallis.

WALLIS   Noël is right, we were inconsiderate. Fruity, perhaps tonight isn't a dancing night. Ernest, you have to accept that my life is different now, and—ohhhh—

WALLIS doubles over in pain and almost falls.

NOËL   How long can you keep us all happy, Wally? The cuckold's cock is in a knot, the king's is standing at attention, the populace is catching on, the prime minister wants to toss the prince, the world is about to go warring again, the balance is about to tip over. Good God, I'm warning you again. I hate this role, I hate it.

EDWARD   Darling?

WALLIS   *(hands pressed to her stomach)* I seem to be losing my famous pep. Someone make a decision. Someone be charming. Someone save the day.

EDWARD   Oh, darling, I forgot. Perhaps this will make you feel better.

RUBY enters. NOËL plays music. RUBY does the runway walk around the apartment, and then EDWARD takes RUBY by the hand and presents it to WALLIS. EDWARD holds up a bracelet.

RUBY A pigeon's blood ruby bracelet, circled by baguette diamonds, designed by Cartier.

WALLIS Ohhhhh…

NOËL Spellbinding.

ERNEST The size, the colour, it must have cost a fortune.

Burmese music. The group is bedazzled and befuddled.

RUBY holds WALLIS's wrist and addresses the group. The SOCIETY CHORUS tiptoes away. RUBY is delicate and feminine except when she's angry.

An awkward silence.

RUBY I am King of Jewels. I am a hundred million years old.

WALLIS There are times I feel at least that.

RUBY Wrung from the earth by slaves, the famous royal Padamyar Ngamauk ruby, stolen by the British in 1884.

WALLIS   I'm American, we never steal.

RUBY   It's blood that matters.

WALLIS   Wait. Royal? David gave me a *royal* ruby?

RUBY   No common blood has ever worn me!

WALLIS   I'm from Baltimore and my mother ran a boarding
              house.

RUBY   When you wear me, a mist will be about you, the
              colour of passion. Each jewel he gives will increase
              his love. You will have powers.

WALLIS   I'm so sick of all these predictions. Where have they
              gotten me? All right, a great boyfriend but—

RUBY   Look into the depths of my red-blood heart.

              RUBY exits.

WALLIS   Ooooh, so beautiful.

NOËL   There's not a woman in the world who could resist.
              Is there?

              Music. NOËL *takes the bracelet from* EDWARD
              and dangles it in front of WALLIS. EDWARD, *Lord*

FALDERAL, and ERNEST fade into the shadows. The apartment disappears.

Be careful, Wallis. For all my warnings, you must beware of me as well. It's time to lead you deeper inside this country, if you are ever to know and feel it. Who knows, the landscape is said to be very healing for ulcers and other gastric complaints…

SCENE TWELVE

THE DEATH OF THE KING

Buckingham Palace, 1935. The KING is lying in the bath chair, surrounded by BERTIE, ELIZABETH, the QUEEN, and a DOCTOR (NOËL). The KING's breath rattles dramatically.

DOCTOR   He's on the verge of death, ma'am.

QUEEN   Yes, I can see that.

DOCTOR   If he dies before midnight, the announcement will be in the morning papers, the *Times* and so on. If he dies later, the king's death will have to be announced in the afternoon tabloids. Not very dignified.

QUEEN   No, not dignified.

KING   Don't kill me yet, wait until I see that cad.

DOCTOR   What's that, sir?

KING   *(bellowing)* I said, don't kill me yet—

BERTIE   I c-can't believe he's not here.

ELIZABETH   He's with that woman, I can feel it. Like poison in the air.

KING   I hope my eldest son never becomes king, never has children, and that nothing will keep Bertie and Elizabeth from the throne.

> EDWARD *enters.* WALLIS *stands in a spotlight and watches.*

BERTIE   Stop, f-father. You're cursing h-him. And me.

QUEEN   David, where have you been?

WALLIS   David, don't let them make you feel small.

EDWARD   I was in my garden trying to feel England. To listen to it. To the ley lines of Stonehenge, to the Druid circles, to the tiniest clutch of periwinkle in a wood.

QUEEN   Control yourself. Listen to God.

EDWARD   My family, generations of kings, spilling royal blood
          and common blood, poured into the earth. I can feel
          them goading me on! Be a man! Snarl, bite, fight,
          crush!

KING   Members of the royal family are like so many planets
          revolving around the monarch sun—

DOCTOR   We're going to end his suffering soon.

KING   Don't kill me yet—

WALLIS   Now. Talk straight with them now, before it's too late.

KING   David has been breaking the laws of royal astronomy.

EDWARD   Mother, if I am to fulfill the arduous duties of
          kingship I need someone beside me who—

QUEEN   You need to prepare yourself for the life that is to
          come. For the changes in all aspects of your routine.

EDWARD   Yes, of course.

KING   Where is he? Is he wearing those bloody... plus fours?

EDWARD   Father, I wanted to tell you about Mrs. Simp—

KING   Who?

QUEEN   Do not mention that woman's name in this house.

ELIZABETH   Palace.

WALLIS   You over-dressed pudding.

QUEEN   All right then, palace.

EDWARD   *(to KING)* I tried to tell you before but—

ELIZABETH   This is cruel. Now he's too sick to respond you're
             finally going to talk to him. David, you must break
             her spell. Do it now, when you are on the verge of
             great power.

EDWARD   She has given me my life.

QUEEN   I gave you your life.

EDWARD   Father, I cannot live without her. I cannot face
             what is to come without her. You don't know her,
             she's… real.

KING   Duty, that's all there is… duty… duty… duty…

EDWARD   Tell my mother you love her. For once tell my mother
             you love—

QUEEN   Control yourself!

ELIZABETH   He's right. There's not enough love. There's not enough love in this room!

QUEEN   Bertie, control your wife.

BERTIE   Dear—

DOCTOR   Ma'am, I think it's time. *(retrieves a large syringe)* Five hundred milligrams of cocaine.

EDWARD   What are you doing?

QUEEN   We are going to end his suffering.

EDWARD   But you can't just—

KING   Oh yes they can. One shot of cocaine and it's all over.

WALLIS   No. It's a bad omen. Don't let them kill him.

> *The DOCTOR gives the injection. EDWARD tries to stop him.*

EDWARD   Noooo!

> *The QUEEN and ELIZABETH hold EDWARD back.*

KING   Are you still afraid of me? Eh? How is the empire?

EDWARD   The empire is thriving, sir.

KING   Good. I hope… we suck… every… penny… we…
        can… out… of… it… before… it… all… turns…
        to… bollocks…

        A huge, rattling breath, then silence.

QUEEN   The king is dead. Long live the king.

        All get on their knees before EDWARD.

EDWARD *(in tears)* Oh my God. It's started. Wallis! Help me.

        WALLIS *appears before* EDWARD.

WALLIS   (*curtsying*) Your Highness.

EDWARD   Do you think I'll make a good king?

WALLIS   I think you could light up this land like a firecracker.

EDWARD   That's my girl. As my first act as king, I will turn the
                clocks in this palace to the right time!

QUEEN   You can't do that. Your father always kept the clocks
                half an hour ahead, so we would never be late.

WALLIS   You're king. Do what you want!

EDWARD   Change the clocks!

BERTIE   Good for you, brother. (*shakes* EDWARD's *hand*) I
                always hated those bloody clocks.

                *The sound of clocks chiming. The royal family
                remain·frozen on their knees.*

WALLIS   Go on, what else?

EDWARD   I want to tear down the mouldy old draperies, I want
                to let in some light, I want to make noise!

                EDWARD *tears down draperies, horrible paintings
                topple to the ground.* WALLIS *joins in.*

WALLIS   Open the windows!

EDWARD   Throw out the chamber orchestra!

ELIZABETH   He's smothered her with rubies, she's dripping with
                 emeralds.

WALLIS   Fire the cook. Modernize the menu.

ELIZABETH   The cook has worked for us for thirty years, you'd
                 throw her in the street?

                 *The sound of jazz overcomes the sound of chiming
                 clocks.*

EDWARD   I will herald a new era. I will bring change, light,
                 and peace to this land. And, my God, Wallis will be
                 at my side.

                 The music stops dead.

WALLIS   The king is dead, long live the king. Club sandwiches
                 for everyone!

                 Music: "Dance Little Lady Dance."

                 Blackout.

                 Intermission. Serve martinis.

ACT TWO
SCENE ONE

ON THE YAHLIN

Music: "We'll Make Hay While the Sun Shines."
Bright sunlight. The sound of waves. NOËL *Coward,*
Lady COLEFAX, *Von* RIBBENTROP, *and the* DEBUTANTE
stand facing the water. All wear sunglasses.

NOËL *and* WALLIS *stroll by themselves.* EDWARD
stands by himself, wearing a checked scarf, look-
ing out to sea.

FALDERAL   Muffy, isn't it time for another cocktail?

COLEFAX   Don't be silly, Fruity, we just had one.

DEBUTANTE   It's very exciting. All of Britain is split; it's the war of
            the roses.

FALDERAL   The Roundheads and the Cavaliers. I support
            our king.

NOËL   But can you support the future queen?

COLEFAX   I'll die before I curtsy to Wallis Simpson.

FALDERAL   But we can't side with the palace. So dowdy, so out
               of touch.

COLEFAX   Parliament will resign en masse if he marries her.

FALDERAL   For God's sake, poor Bertie is in no shape to take
               over the empire.

COLEFAX   How the royal family must hate her.

DEBUTANTE   What do you wear during a revolution?

COLEFAX   Go simple, with a lot of beads.

WALLIS   (to EDWARD) We can't hide on this boat forever.

EDWARD   Ship, actually. Or "yacht," if you prefer.

               EDWARD *stands on his head.*

WALLIS   I don't care. It's like we're going round and round…
               And that chatter, it's making me seasick. I'm all over
               the newspapers in the States; they're ready to crown
               me or hang me—we have to make decisions.

EDWARD   We are above their lies.

WALLIS   Look at reality.

EDWARD   I don't like reality.

WALLIS   That's your luxury.

EDWARD   No, actually, I think it's a good thing. Look at war. Let's say, darling, that the two of us went to a grand hotel, say the Ritz, and stayed in bed for a whole year. We invite the press and say that we are loving for peace.

WALLIS   You mean us bonking away in a hotel would keep the world from going to war?

EDWARD   A suggestion. If everyone did like us, there would be no war.

          He jogs around the deck.

          It makes as much sense as anything else.

FALDERAL Do we really have to go overland to Sarajevo? Wars are always starting there. Let's forget it and just sail on to—

COLEFAX   Italy. And we could have lunch there. Oh, is that supposed to be a secret?

NOËL   That we're having lunch?

COLEFAX   No, that we're here at all. Disguising all this diplomacy with fun. Or is it fun?

FALDERAL   It's no secret that Mrs. Simpson's here.

DEBUTANTE   And she's fun. Or is she, anymore?

> *The* SOCIETY CHORUS *crosses the stage.*

FALDERAL   He might actually give up a kingdom for her.

> *The sound of thousands of people cheering and shouting.*

COLEFAX   Look at the crowds, down by the water.

FALDERAL   The Italians are shouting something. What is it?

> *The Italians on shore shout "Viva l'amoure!" "Viva l'amoure!"*

NOËL   *Viva l'amoure.*

DEBUTANTE   It's so romantic.

EDWARD   Long live love. Thousands of them, lining the shore!

FALDERAL   Incredible!

EDWARD   They're on our side. The people are on the side of love.

NOËL   Of obsession and dependence.

DEBUTANTE   Of the love story of the century.

EDWARD   Wave, darling. We'll be all right as long as—

WALLIS   As long as what?

EDWARD   As long as the personal doesn't become political.

> *They all wave to the crowds. The sound of cheering rises, then abrupt silence.*

SCENE TWO

BERLIN, 1935

HITLER is watching films of WALLIS and EDWARD. The light flickers eerily on his face.

HITLER   No. No. No! We don't want to make sense, we want to make magic. All politics comes from the soul, from the feelings, and from the clothes. Look at Mrs. Simpson. What a queen she will make. Look at that face; she knows power, she wants power. What style.

I have saving the world on my mind! How to clean up the streets of Jews, criminals, gypsies, left-wing intellectuals, and dirty homosexuals. How to stop giving money to retarded people and unmarried mothers. England should be on our side. That little Aryan king understands. But she, she is the key.

SCENE THREE

THREE BUGS IN A RUG

Music: "I'm Putting All My Eggs In One Basket."
WALLIS *and* EDWARD *are in bed.*

EDWARD   My family won't speak to me. I've tried everything;
            the entire establishment is against me.

WALLIS   Nanny's very angry. You need a spanking—a real one,
            with a whip, royal blood running down your little
            white bum. Be a man. Fight. Stand up to them. Get
            a PR agent for Christ's sake. You're so popular, the
            people will support you. Go to the people. Get on
            the radio. Show all those stuffed shirts who's who.

EDWARD   I will not do anything ungentlemanly or ignoble.

WALLIS   Then you'll lose. David, if you're not king, who will
            you be?

EDWARD   A free human being with the power to influence
            world affairs without the weighty chains of monarchy.

WALLIS   Darling, you can't abdicate and eat it too.

            They both crack up laughing.

            Enter NOËL.

NOËL	Excellent to hear you're both in good humour. The maid seems to have disappeared.
WALLIS	Everyone's deserted us. Climb in, Noël, we have no secrets from you.
NOËL	That's not true.
WALLIS	No, it's not true.
EDWARD	Perhaps it is true.
NOËL	Men of my persuasion love Wallis.
EDWARD	Everyone loves Wallis. If only my family would meet her—
WALLIS	You have to fight for me. Right, Noël?
NOËL	Fight.
WALLIS	Right.
NOËL	Sir, I've always felt we have a great deal in common.
EDWARD	We both love Wallis?
WALLIS	Shut up, Noël.
EDWARD	Be nice to Noël, darling.

WALLIS   *(to* NOËL*)* You've got it wrong, Noël.

NOËL   You love checked shirts, for instance.

WALLIS   Lots of men loved checked shirts.

NOËL   You are high-strung and vaguely artistic.

EDWARD   My curse and my blessing.

WALLIS   What's that?

           *Shouting from a crowd outside. The jewels play
           the crowd.*

SAPPHIRE   We support you, sir!

CROWD   Yeahhhhh!

DIAMOND   Down with the whore!

RUBY   Save our king!

SAPPHIRE   Save our king!

DIAMOND   Sir, you marry who you want!

EDWARD   Such a lot of noise.

NOËL   You see, sir, a certain kind of man loves loud, funny women who aren't pretty but are very good company. Often these women are very… large.

WALLIS   I'm not large and I'm not that funny.

EDWARD   What are you getting at, old man?

              EMERALD, *pretending to be a newsboy, crosses in front of the bed.*

EMERALD   Constitutional Crisis! Constitutional Crisis! Will the King Wed Wally?

              NOËL, WALLIS, and EDWARD ignore the sounds. More chanting from the crowd. It gets louder. The group on the bed seem not to hear. The SOCIETY CHORUS gathers in a corner, chatting excitedly.

WALLIS   He's saying that perhaps you don't want to marry any woman.

EDWARD   I cannot live without Wallis. I will not live without Wallis.

              Increased shouting from crowd outside.

JEWELS   Abdication means revolution!
              Abdication means revolution!
              Abdication means revolution!

A brick smashes through the window.

WALLIS   Ah! What's that?

NOËL   A brick, I believe.

WALLIS   A brick? What's next? Burn me at the stake?

EDWARD   I'm calling the palace guard.

WALLIS   I have to get out of here. I'll never be queen; they're going to kill me.

EDWARD   I won't let them.

WALLIS   Then be a man.

NOËL   You can't just stop, Wallis.

WALLIS   Yes I can. David, we've had a very special time, which I will treasure till my dying day, but I now have to leave. Noël? Help me pack.

     NOËL doesn't move.

NOËL   I'd rather watch.

EDWARD   I won't let you go.

WALLIS   A woman tried to throw acid in my face for stealing her king. You people are crazy. I'm getting out of here; this whole place is going to blow.

EDWARD   I will close the ports, alert the authorities, you are going nowhere without my say-so.

WALLIS   You'll marry some mangy foreign princess like you should have done years ago. Believe me, I can be replaced.

EDWARD   I will not let you go! Ever! Do you hear me! I will find you, I will follow you to the ends of the earth. They say it is weakness for a man to love this much, they call it obsession, but I say it makes me strong.

WALLIS   David, you and I have had a very special time—

EDWARD   I will stand up to them. The archbishop, my mother, the prime minister, the whole lot. I can still do it, I can make you queen.

WALLIS   You're a wimp. You're a faggot. I hate your love. I'll kill it.

EDWARD   You can't, peachums, you can't.

WALLIS   Look at me. Inside me is the blackest queen you ever
             saw. Everything they say is true. I'm out for what I
             can get. I did it for the money.

EDWARD   I do have the power to look inside you. And I see
             goodness.

WALLIS   I'm begging you—the more you love me, the crueller
             you are.

EDWARD   This is how modern men will be.

WALLIS   I'm old fashioned. Treat me like shit.

EDWARD   You are a modern woman, and that is why you will
             recognize an offer—as they say in America—that you
             can't refuse. A promise.

             (on his knees) You will never be alone. I will love you
             in old age, in illness, in the face of all tests and trials.
             I will never blame you, never turn on you, never
             betray you. Until your death and beyond, you will
             be loved as deeply and as completely as any woman
             has ever been loved. (gives WALLIS a box) I had this
             made for you, darling.

             EDWARD bows and exits.

NOËL   There's going to be a war, and it will be horrible. I've
             had a vision, and you, Wallis, are in that vision. It's

almost as if you'd started the whole thing. You're the kind of woman who starts wars.

WALLIS   Wallis of Troy?

WALLIS opens the box. DIAMOND enters.

DIAMOND   An African-diamond-encrusted heart pin topped with a ruby crown—

WALLIS   Oh!

NOËL   I've been your friend, and now I realize you have no concept of love. It's something you're missing, like a tooth or an appendix.

DIAMOND   The jewelled heart beats. *(making the sound of a heart beating)* Pah pum. Pah pum. Pah pum.

NOËL   That heart of little stones beats more fully than your own.

WALLIS   What are you saying?

NOËL   I don't know.

WALLIS   You've been my only real friend.

NOËL says nothing.

You're still my friend.

NOËL says nothing.

Aren't you?

NOËL You weren't supposed to go this far. You were just supposed to bring in a little fresh air.

WALLIS I'm a tornado, not a little English breeze. I destroy everything in my wake.

NOËL Tell me you love him.

WALLIS Why should I tell you anything?

NOËL Because I am asking you.

WALLIS pins the jewelled heart above her own.

WALLIS I will have a kingdom and I will be queen.

The wind blows…

SCENE FOUR

THE ABDICATION

Gregorian chants. Smoke. Candles. Incense. A throne. The ARCHBISHOP, in a huge vaulted hat, stands behind the throne, crown in hand. The QUEEN, ELIZABETH, and BERTIE enter in a procession. EDWARD sits on the throne and gives his speech.

EDWARD   A few hours ago, I discharged my last duty as king and emperor.

WALLIS   No! Oh no. No no no no no!

> *WALLIS throws down chairs. Crashes things to the ground.*

EDWARD   I have tried for twenty-five years to serve, but I have found it impossible to carry the heavy burden of responsibility without the help and support of the woman I love.

ARCHBISHOP   Edward the Eighth, Emperor, King, Lord of the Dominions, Protector of the Faith, you are dethroned, defrocked, cast out!

> *A specific crash of thunder.*

Wallis Simpson, American commoner, double divorcee, you will walk in humiliation for the rest of your days. You will take your place among the rag-tag dukes and exiled duchesses of our age. And your common name will be Windsor.

EDWARD   My brother has one matchless blessing, enjoyed by so many of you and not bestowed on me—a happy home with his wife and children. I now lay down my burden. And now we all have a new king. I wish him, and you, his people, happiness and prosperity, with all my heart. God bless you all. God save the king.

> *EDWARD bows to* BERTIE, *then moves to* WALLIS'*s side. He hands* WALLIS *a blue wedding veil. They exchange rings as they are cursed. The coronation continues.*

QUEEN   No member of the royal family will receive you or "that woman." We will not attend your wedding, we will not send any presents.

BERTIE   Damn you. You have sent me to an early g-grave. Let that be on your h-h-head.

ELIZABETH   As the queen mother, the people will love my kindness, but for the woman who will cause my husband untold agonies, I will show no mercy. I will make certain you are denied royal status. No one will ever curtsy to you.

QUEEN   You have no family. I am no longer your mother, your brothers are no longer your brothers.

ARCHBISHOP You have no country. Be gone from this land until the day you die.

> BERTIE *sits on the throne. The throne is wheeled away with* BERTIE *in it. They exit in a solemn procession as the* ARCHBISHOP *swears him in.*

WALLIS &
EDWARD   Noooooooooo!

SCENE FIVE

THE VOID

> A *cold wind blows.* WALLIS *and* EDWARD *sit on suitcases on an empty stage.*

EDWARD   *(gasping)* I can't seem to catch my breath.

WALLIS   *(gasping)* Neither can I.

EDWARD   My limbs are heavy.

WALLIS   *(still fighting for air)* The air is… thinner in the real world. There's less… oxygen. Less everything. I'll…

get used to it quicker. I used to be used to the real
world.

EDWARD   And the servants to carry the luggage, and make
arrangements?

       WALLIS stares.

    Aides, attachés, assistants, men at arms?

WALLIS   Have you ever made your own bed? Ever dressed
yourself? Waited for a train? Worried about money?

EDWARD   I've often dressed myself.

WALLIS   Oh my God.

CHORUS   We never liked her,
we never invited her,
we never laughed at her rebarbative humour,
we never had cocktails,
never ever danced with her.
There is no mystery,
no mystery of Wallis Simpson.
No charisma, no lesson, nothing to be learned,
sometimes things just eff up.

EDWARD   I can't decide where we should live.

WALLIS   I can't decide who we should be.

EDWARD   When things settle down, we'll go back to England.
           Then I'll be given some important diplomatic service
           and we will be an influence in the world.

WALLIS   They're not going to let us back. Ever.

EDWARD   Darling, it's our honeymoon.

WALLIS   Coward. You should have stood up to them. I would
           have done it.

EDWARD   I left as a king and a gentleman should.

WALLIS   My skin is wrinkling, there's a horrible cleft between
           my brows like I've been hit with an axe. I need a
           facelift. Three facelifts.

EDWARD   I've taken you into the void, haven't I? I see it now.

WALLIS   There's nowhere to run.

EDWARD   I will make it up to you. If it takes my last breath,
           I'm going to make it worth it that you met and loved
           Edward VIII.

WALLIS   Ex-Edward VIII.

           Von RIBBENTROP enters.

RIBBENTROP *(bowing)* Your Royal Highness. Duchess.

WALLIS   Count Von Ribbentrop. What brings you to the void?

RIBBENTROP Sir, your family has treated you and your new wife with contempt, but I know a place where you will still be regarded as the sovereign. What is the answer to sadness and loss? It is splendour, it is glory. I can take you to a kingdom that understands the role of good blood. Come with me and I will tell you of our prophesies…

> EDWARD *and* WALLIS *follow* RIBBENTROP *as the sound of marching feet fills the air. Martial music. Cheering crowds.*

SCENE SIX

PUBLIC RELATIONS

> *Buckingham Palace, 1936. The sound of a cold wind blowing. The* QUEEN, ELIZABETH, BERTIE, *and* NOËL *Coward.* ELIZABETH *carries a large glass of gin.*

NOËL   I'm honoured to have been asked for my help. "Public relations" is such an American phenomena, but I might have a few suggestions—

ELIZABETH Do you know what they're singing in the streets? "Hark the herald angels sing, Wallis Simpson's nicked our king."

NOËL   Popularity is an odd thing. I've always been very
             popular, but to create popularity—

ELIZABETH   You've always been great friends with Mrs. Simpson,
             haven't you, Mr. Coward?

NOËL   I wouldn't say friends. Acquaintances.

QUEEN   I have no idea what David can be thinking.

ELIZABETH   He is your son.

QUEEN   Why do you assume the umbilical cord is still intact
             like some kind of telephone wire? I don't know him.

ELIZABETH   And why not?

QUEEN   Because I am as cold as this unnatural winter. Is that
             what you want to hear? Is that what Wallis Simpson
             thinks?

ELIZABETH   I don't care what she thinks.

NOËL   If we could keep our eye on the concept of publicity—

QUEEN   (to ELIZABETH) Oh, yes you do. You think about her
             all the time.

ELIZABETH   Yes. She gave David a kind of strength, and I need
             to know how she did it.

QUEEN   He was weak! Weak enough to give up a kingdom.

NOËL   The right photographs, that is important, reinforcing an image of stability and family.

QUEEN   (*glancing at* BERTIE) The king is very timid, Mr. Coward. A day at the photographers would do him in.

NOËL   Well then, perhaps Queen Elizabeth would consider posing alone, ma'am, you are definitely an asset—your smile—

ELIZABETH   We'll never be rid of them. David wears a new hat and he's on the front page, while Bertie—

NOËL   The front page, that is the key—

QUEEN   Bertie is a plodder, and he will sire plodders, and that is how the monarchy will survive.

ELIZABETH   How dare you.

NOËL   Perhaps I should come another time—

QUEEN   Don't "how dare you" me. I was queen when you were a little bit of crinoline in your mother's dim mind.

BERTIE   D-David is right. He has a g-grasp of world affairs. He's right about the danger of war. It w-will destroy our world.

NOËL   You see, here is strength, here is resolution, we must get the message out—

ELIZABETH   Bertie, you must stop talking to David, stop listening to his advice.

BERTIE   He is my brother.

ELIZABETH   He is bewitched.

                I need a drink. *(realizes she already has one)* Oh.

QUEEN   I'll have one too.

NOËL   Well, if drinks are being served—

BERTIE   My b-brother has doomed me—

QUEEN   Mr. Coward, do you have any information that might help us?

NOËL   I believe they are going to visit Hitler.

ELIZABETH   You see? God is on our side.

SCENE SEVEN

WALLIS AND THE DEVIL

Nazi Germany. Harsh lighting. Sound: magical notes. HITLER *is painting at an easel and humming a sweet tune.* WALLIS *enters.*

HITLER   The duchess! Please come in. No, don't be afraid. I've sent everyone away.

WALLIS   I'm not afraid.

HITLER   I thought perhaps you would like to see what I do when I'm not leading my country. I've never liked the Impressionists. Everything ruled by the sun. They don't see the shadows, the little cottage in the woods. They consider me unsubtle, but look at this—full of subtlety.

WALLIS   It looks like a map of the world.

HITLER   *(innocently)* Does it?

WALLIS   I'm not exactly sure why I'm here. The Duke of Windsor is off somewhere… I know what he wants to say to you—

HITLER   But what do you want to say to me?

WALLIS   That you're greedy. Yes, every other major country has an empire, and you should probably have one too, but even after Versailles, not that much of an empire—

HITLER   Do you know why I wanted to see you? Because we have the same eyes.

WALLIS   Mine are blue.

HITLER   And what are those eyes looking at? The future! What do you think when you parade through the streets on your royal progress, thousands of people cheering? Most people would think, oh, I'm too unworthy, but no. You say: "I deserve it!"

WALLIS   Not at all. I smile, because I know it's a joke. It's on them and it's on me. I deserve it because I'm willing to go through with the joke. That's what you Fascists are missing: a sense of humour.

HITLER   How are you doing? Are you happy you got kicked out? That you got treated like a piece of shit? Are you happy they tried to kill you, smear you, that they called you a slut?

WALLIS   No.

HITLER   When I get to England, I am going to sink down into its soggy, mushy green grass, and I will kiss the ground. I see that island the way you see it, as a stranger.

WALLIS   They'll never let you in. You think that island is real. But it isn't.

HITLER   Nonsense. And who will rule beside me? You. Because you understand power.

WALLIS   I don't understand it. I just attract it.

HITLER   Liar! You don't belong with that delicate blond boy. You want me. Look into my eyes. You are a Nazi.

WALLIS   I can feel something from you. A force. It pulls me right from my guts. Is it soul? Why do you look like the most beautiful man in the world? What is that colour around you? It's… magenta. Not the pale pink of the empire, but a fiery, fiery rose.

HITLER   Pink? Are you certain the colour is not pink?

WALLIS   It's the common sense I like, common sense mixed with soul, mixed with sex, with power, mixed with… the chosen.

HITLER   Yes!

WALLIS   You want to be chosen, and you want to choose who's chosen.

HITLER   All politics come from the soul, from the feelings and from the clothes. Look at you. What a queen you will make. It is about beauty, about blood, about style!

> WALLIS *is drawn towards* HITLER, *deeply aroused by his speech.*

WALLIS   I want to suck your vision. I want to suck your sureness, your mind, and your blood. Take me right here, right now.

> HITLER *fumbles with his trousers.*

HITLER   Just give me a second.

> *She lies on the floor.*

WALLIS   Right on this beautifully painted map of the world. I'm lying on England and France, I'm reaching for Russia, and my stomach is all over Yugoslavia.

HITLER   Patience is not my virtue.

WALLIS   You'll fill up the hole in my guts. Take me. I knew a land once, and that land betrayed me. I would have learned to care—

HITLER   Enough talk. Action. Blitzkrieg!

WALLIS   Just one more little thing—

HITLER   What? What?

WALLIS   Your eyes are small.

HITLER   No, they're big, look how big.

WALLIS   Not like mine at all. A tiny flaw, really. I can't help
             thinking of David's eyes… No, I won't think of that.
             Keep your pants on, just give me a minute. What
             was that change in the air? I was there. I could have
             a new kingdom—

HITLER   Don't play with me, lady. I warn you.

WALLIS   You're going to lose. You can tell because of the
             moustache. You should let it grow, or shave it off.
             Either a man has a moustache or he doesn't. You're
             going to lose.

HITLER   Because of my moustache?

WALLIS   It's a failure of style.

             *EDWARD enters and gives the Fascist salute. Count
             Von RIBBENTROP takes a picture. Flash.*

EDWARD   Herr Hitler. *(to WALLIS)* Darling, I was worried.

HITLER	Past and future King! I kneel to you. Knight me, do that thing with the sword, I love all that stuff. How do you think you can keep a woman like her if you have no power?
EDWARD	The thought has occurred to me.
HITLER	I want your wife.
EDWARD	Well, I'm sorry, but you can't have her.
WALLIS	David, we have to go.
EDWARD	If we let go of our dance with Herr Hitler, we lose our last bit of leverage on the world stage. There will be no way back, my family will take full control. We will become as shadows.
WALLIS	We're already shadows.
HITLER	Stop all this sensitivity! Take my hand and I will put you back on the throne of England. A real king with real power. A tyrant. Take my hand.
	HITLER reaches out his hand. Bewitched, EDWARD goes towards him and almost takes it…
WALLIS	He's going to lose.
EDWARD	What? Lose? Oh, well then, call our driver.

HITLER   Love. Soul.

               WALLIS and EDWARD move towards HITLER.

               Feelings. Prophesy. Iron. Blood. Magic…

WALLIS   Let's get out of here.

RIBBENTROP Take me with you. Take me.

EDWARD   Sorry, old man, there's no room.

               WALLIS and EDWARD flee.

HITLER   Now!

               World War II begins.

SCENE EIGHT

WORLD WAR II

The sound of bombs, tanks, planes, screaming. After an unbearable crescendo of noise, there is a moment of silence. The SOCIETY CHORUS stands as if honouring the dead. A soldier, covered in blood, lies in ELIZABETH's lap.

ELIZABETH   Now is my time, our time, "just we four." This is no
time for style, this is a moment for real courage. My
heart is growing so much, my breasts are inflating;
I have milk enough for this whole land. I have milk
for the dead. Is that power? Is that what it does? I
am the beloved Queen Mother. My Elizabeth will
reign, and as I roll up her little ringlets, I teach her
how to rule with a love of tradition that will make
her invulnerable. Wallis is barren. The Windsors will
never threaten this dynasty with their cheap flash.
Oh no, they will never curtsy to you, my scrawny
duchess. You have shown your colours.

SCENE NINE

THE BAHAMAS

*The jewels sing a calypso song to the tune of "Love,
Love Alone."*

JEWELS   It's love, love alone,
Caused King Edward to leave the throne.
I know King Edward was noble and great
But it's love that caused him to abdicate.

I know my mama she's gonna grieve
He said, "I cannot help it but I'm bound to leave.
You can take me throne, you can take me crown
But leave me Mrs. Simpson to renown."

It's love, love alone,
That caused King Edward to leave the throne.

> *A few wilted palm trees. Piles of suitcases litter the stage, still unpacked.* WALLIS *consults a long list.*

> EDWARD *enters.*

WALLIS   What a climate. The royal family has sent us to hell for our many sins. Even my makeup's melting.

EDWARD   I did get a job as governor of the Bahamas, didn't I, darling? Didn't I?

WALLIS   I sent out the invitations to our dinner party weeks ago, and no one has replied.

EDWARD   The distance.

WALLIS   I offered to pay their fare, put them up—

EDWARD   Before the abdication—

WALLIS   Don't say that word!

EDWARD   What word?

WALLIS   You know what word.

EDWARD   Abdicate?

WALLIS   Stop it.

EDWARD   Abdicate abdicate abdicate. I had to abdicate—

WALLIS   Stop talking about the past!

EDWARD   Sorry, darling.

WALLIS   Stop apologizing!

EDWARD   Sorry.

WALLIS   No one is coming to my party.

EDWARD   Let's be gay. Open the champagne, we'll banter about
                as we used to.

WALLIS   There's no audience. What is the sound of two people
                bantering by themselves? The ice is melting. *(to
                DIAMOND)* More ice. We are melting. Soon we'll be
                two expensive puddles of water.

                NOËL enters.

NOËL   I'm tired, Wallis, for the first time in my life. Even my
                jokes are starting to fail. I can see the outside now,
                as if the walls to our kingdom are disappearing, and
                through the holes in the mist I see hordes of badly
                dressed people.

EDWARD   Cocktails?

NOËL   The bourgeoisie are drinking cocktails now.

EDWARD   Democracy creates rule by middle-class taste.

WALLIS   Soon all we'll be eating are hamburgers. *(to NOËL)*
                So you came.

NOËL   I was in the neighbourhood. What are you wearing?

WALLIS   *(wearily)* A dress. What's wrong with it?

NOËL   Nothing. It's just not very…

                EDWARD serves the drinks. DIAMOND assists. The
                three sit on suitcases, fanning themselves.

EDWARD   I always make the best cocktails. Shaken not stirred.

WALLIS   Can you believe that anyone stirs cocktails.

NOËL   Appalling.

                Pause.

WALLIS   Have you seen anybody recently?

NOËL   Who?

WALLIS   Anybody.

NOËL   Not really.

                Pause.

EDWARD   I've been very busy lately.

NOËL   Oh?

EDWARD   Yes. Governing these islands is no easy job.

WALLIS   We work like dogs.

NOËL   Terrible. Or… excellent. That you're busy.

              Pause.

EDWARD   I suppose England is—

WALLIS   Don't talk about that ghastly island.

EDWARD   Of course, you're right.

              Pause.

WALLIS   We love the weather here, the tropics are so bright.

NOËL   Wallis, I—

WALLIS   Yes?

NOËL   I suppose you're blissfully happy.

EDWARD   I have found Wallis to be utterly without faults. The perfect woman.

WALLIS   We're tremendously happy. We're the love story of the century.

EDWARD   When I was king—

WALLIS   Don't talk about the past!

EDWARD   I was just going to offer my opinion on the course of
          the war—

WALLIS   Who cares about your stupid opinions?

EDWARD   Well, my family—

WALLIS   Your family? I curse the House of Windsor. May they
          be brought to their knees by adultery, betrayal, and
          divorce.

          NOËL *stands.*

NOËL   Well. This has been lovely.

EDWARD   Leaving already?

NOËL   I'm on a tour, you see. Doing my bit.

WALLIS   One more cocktail? A green one?

NOËL   Duty calls.

EDWARD   Duty?

WALLIS   Yes, of course. We're madly busy too.

NOËL   You have a husband.

WALLIS   I have to keep it up. The love story of the century—I'm so tired, I have to keep it up.

NOËL   Make that your ambition.

WALLIS   Ambition.

NOËL   Sir. Duchess. See you… anon.

          NOËL exits.

EDWARD   Darling, I—

WALLIS   Go away!

EDWARD   But peachums—

WALLIS   Stuff it.

          The dim light of a tropical night.

EDWARD   Tonight I won't speak of love. I'll light the lamps. They will sparkle like the jewels you've always loved. I used to see you play with them like a child. Speaking, murmuring to them. I haven't seen you do that in such a long time. I'll light the lamps. Lighting your way home.

WALLIS   I need.

EDWARD   What? Tell me. Tell me what you need, Wallis, and
           I will give it to you.

           Silence from WALLIS.

WALLIS   A woman's life can really be a... succession of lives,
           revolving around some compelling challenge... I
           need a kingdom in exile.

           *WALLIS repeats her mantra over and over, her hands
           clenched with effort. Sweat pours down her face.
           Sound: magical notes. The jewels appear and
           create the Kingdom in Exile.*

EDWARD   A kingdom like none has seen before, designed for
           rapture. An entrance hall, all in green...

WALLIS   No, midnight blue, covered in tiny stars.

           *The domed ceiling erupts into thousands of white
           lights.*

EDWARD   Yes!

WALLIS   A long, curving staircase, a carpet of ruby red—

EDWARD   Carpets as thick as grass—

WALLIS   Smells, scents.

EDWARD   Exquisite perfumes follow the visitor, reminding
          them of their first love—

WALLIS   Pools of light, cobwebs of silk, rounded porcelains.
          Shapes that seem to move and dance.

EDWARD   Music that throbs and excites—

WALLIS   *(doubled over)* The food, don't forget… the food—

EDWARD   Sauces so light they seem to float.

EDWARD &
WALLIS   *(in unison)* A symphony of tastes—

WALLIS   Addictive and enchanted.

          *A banquet table appears from the sky. It is
          beautifully set, with tall candles and covered in
          embroidered cloths. Leaves of lettuce curl in velvet
          tendrils around the centrepiece. The salmon is a
          most delicate peach.*

          WALLIS collapses.

EDWARD   We will invite the world to dinner, my dear, and the
          world will die to accept.

SCENE TEN

THE MAD DINNER PARTY

1968. Music: "Jumpin' Jack Flash." The QUEEN, ELIZABETH *(now the Queen Mother),* NOËL *Coward, Lord* FALDERAL, *Lady* COLEFAX, *the* DEBUTANTE, *and Count Von* RIBBENTROP *enter the Kingdom in Exile.*

NOËL   Stunning.

COLEFAX   Enchanted.

FALDERAL   Pagan.

NOËL   There is so much oxygen, I can breathe easily for the first time in years.

COLEFAX   Like another world. She obviously had professional help.

ELIZABETH   That scent reminds me of the first time I was in love—

NOËL   It's not real, of course.

COLEFAX   It's as real as we ever were.

FALDERAL   Our power has faded, but here we have power still.

NOËL   Faded? Speak for yourself. I personally spend a lot of time in Vegas, selling what's left of Faerie to the Americans.

EDWARD   *(toasting)* To the Duchess of Windsor.

ALL   The Duchess of Windsor.

RIBBENTROP The best-dressed woman in the world!

COLEFAX   Fashions fade, style is eternal.

NOËL   What is Von Ribbentrop doing here?

RIBBENTROP What did you expect me to do? Commit suicide? Never have dinner? The devil is dead.

           WALLIS *enters, looking chic.*

WALLIS   There isn't a wealthy dinner table in the world that doesn't contain at least one true Fascist.

COLEFAX   We do love order and discipline.

DEBUTANTE Is that right wing?

COLEFAX   Who knows anymore?

WALLIS   The hardest years in life are those between ten and seventy.

General laughter.

DEBUTANTE Just looking at Wallis makes me want to go shopping. I want to shop and shop.

ELIZABETH How many facelifts do you think she's had?

QUEEN I heard five, but it could be six.

FALDERAL He still follows her every movement with his eyes. How does she do it?

NOËL That diamond has so many carats it's almost a turnip.

WALLIS So you came.

NOËL Style is my master.

WALLIS Mistress.

EDWARD Where have you been, old chap?

NOËL Working for a living, it's dreadful.

DEBUTANTE *(to NOËL)* So you play the piano, do you?

NOËL Good God—the future.

ELIZABETH I hope you've suffered all these years. Bertie is dead. You killed my husband.

WALLIS   Well we're even. You ruined my life.

DEBUTANTE We're trying to work out who ruined whose life.

WALLIS   I ruined the duke's life.

EDWARD   No, darling, I ruined your life.

WALLIS   Terribly sorry. I stand corrected.

          General laughter.

COLEFAX   *(to DEBUTANTE)* Never before has a man given up so
          much for so little.

DEBUTANTE She never loved him.

WALLIS   The trouble with women is they get all excited about
          nothing—and then they marry him.

          General laughter.

EDWARD   Darling, your kingdom is a success. *(toasting)* To the
          Duchess of Windsor!

ALL   The Duchess of Windsor!

          Music. "Jumpin' Jack Flash."

WALLIS   I've learned a new dance called the Fruge.

NOËL   Horrible.

FALDERAL   You can't just rock, you have to be able to roll.

WALLIS   You may look a little foolish, but it's a wise woman
            who knows she's a fool.

NOËL   She's determined not to lose.

COLEFAX   Is that admirable?

NOËL   It must be.

WALLIS   Everyone on your feet.

            All rise.

            Now people dance without touching each other,
            which may or may not be a better idea. Your legs go
            in one direction and your body in another. Then do
            whatever your body tells you to do. That's what I've
            always done anyway.

DEBUTANTE   Rock and roll is music from the neck down.

NOËL   Whereas my music is for the face only.

            General laughter.

            Everyone starts dancing.

Suddenly EDWARD *clutches his throat.*

EDWARD   *(cries in pain)* Ahhh!

WALLIS   David? What is it?

EDWARD   Sorry, everyone, it's my cancer. We may have to wait... for that... dance.

CHORUS   *(a sound of disappointment)* Ohhhhhhhhh

> EDWARD *crawls onto the banquet table, which becomes his deathbed. The guests walk away except for* NOËL *Coward, who watches the next scene.*

SCENE ELEVEN

EDWARD'S DEATH

> EDWARD *lies on the banquet table,* WALLIS *sits beside him, holding his hand.*

EDWARD   *(in pain, almost blind)* Wallis? Wallis?

WALLIS   I'm here.

EDWARD   Where are you?

WALLIS   Wally's here and she's never going to go away.

EDWARD   I want some peaches.

WALLIS   *(coarse and loud)* Get him some peaches!

EDWARD   Wallis?

WALLIS   Yes, my dear—

EDWARD   Hold tight, Wallis.

WALLIS   I'm holding tight, darling, David. Darling.

EDWARD   Yes, we held tight.

WALLIS   We did, we held tight.

EDWARD   Love?

WALLIS   Yes, love?

EDWARD   Love?

WALLIS   Yes, yes love?

EDWARD   Peaches, you are peaches.

WALLIS   You're so silly. You are silly.

EDWARD   *(moans in pain)* Wallis! Wallis!

WALLIS   Nanny's very angry with you. You're not eating. You
            need a spanking.

EDWARD   Mama. Mama?

WALLIS   Your mama was a cold bitch who never gave you
            anything.

EDWARD   I can't breathe.

WALLIS   Bad baby. Bad, naughty, dirty boy.

EDWARD   You do… love me, don't you.

WALLIS   David—

EDWARD   It doesn't matter. Nothing will ever part us, not even
            death.

WALLIS   Dear, what is it you've loved about me? What is it?

EDWARD   Your… innocence.

                  EDWARD *dies*.

WALLIS   (*hits* EDWARD *across the chest*) David? David?

NOËL   Wallis, it's over. The king is dead. Long live the
            queen.

WALLIS shakes NOËL off with a cry like a caged animal.

WALLIS   You tricked me, you all tricked me.

NOËL   Wallis? It's time to begin the auction again. All of your precious things will be sold. You can't stop it this time.

WALLIS   I am the twentieth century, when love was too late and betrayals rang wide and there was no pity. I am the twentieth century, brutal and greedy and fun— but I loved him. Take my jewels, maestro, sell them high; make a bidding war to end all wars. I am going to dance.

          WALLIS dances like a very old puppet.

          The jewels enter. Flashbulbs. The sound of a boisterous auction crowd. The gavel pounding.

NOËL   And what am I bid… for the jewels of Wallis Simpson?

          Lights fade slowly to black.

          Curtain.

          Curtain Call: "The Black Bottom."

Playwright/actor/producer Linda Griffiths has written, acted, and developed theatre for over three decades. Her plays include *Maggie and Pierre*, *O.D. On Paradise*, *Jessica*, *The Darling Family*, *Alien Creature*, and *Age of Arousal*. She has been the recipient of numerous awards for acting and writing, including five Dora Mavor Moore Awards, two Chalmers Canadian Play Awards, a Betty Mitchell Award, and has twice been nominated for the Governor General's Literary Award. As an actor she's received an ACTRA Award for her work on *Empire Inc.* and Los Angeles's Actors Guild of America award for her performance in John Sayles's *Lianna*. Griffiths's company Duchess Productions has developed much of her work including her newest solo show *The Last Dog of War*. Her most recent works are *HeavenAbove/HeavenBelow*, a sequel to the *The Darling Family*, and *Games*. Griffiths received the Barker Fairley Visitorship at U of T in 2011 and was awarded the Playwrights Guild of Canada's Lifetime Award in 2013.

Printed and bound in Canada by Marquis Book Printing, Montreal

Cover design by Leah Renihan
Book design by Blake Sproule

Photo Credits:
Cover: Linda Griffiths as Margaret Trudeau by Glen Erikson, Linda Griffiths as Wallis Simpson by Trudie Lee.

Page 7: Linda Griffiths with Pierre Trudeau © Copyright John Mahler/Getstock.com.

Maggie and Pierre: All photos of Linda Griffiths from *Maggie and Pierre* are by Glen Erikson. All resonable efforts have been made to contact the photographer. If any reader can provide information as to his whereabouts, please contact Playwrights Canada Press.

The Duchess: All photos from *The Duchess* are by Cylla von Tiedemann.

Page 130: Linda Griffiths as Wallis Simpson.

Page 178: From lef to right, Donna Goodhand as Elizabeth, Jonathan Wilson as Edward, Jennifer Phipps as the queen, David Fox as the king, Louis Negen as the doctor, and John Jarvis as Bertie.

Page 185: Louis Negen as Noël Coward, Linda Griffiths as Wallis Simpson, and Jonathan Wilson as Edward.

Page 214: Linda Griffiths as Wallis Simpson and Jonathan Wilson as Edward.

 **PLAYWRIGHTS CANADA PRESS**

202-269 Richmond St. W.
Toronto, ON
M5V 1X1

416.703.0013
info@playwrightscanada.com
www.playwrightscanada.com